OVERTHINKING

Achieve Your Goals & Reach Your Fullest Potential

(How to Stop Worrying, Negative Thinking and
Healing From Negative Thoughts)

Juan Vaughn

I0106452

Published by Knowledge Icons

Juan Vaughn

Overthinking: Achieve Your Goals & Reach Your Fullest Potential (How to Stop Worrying, Negative Thinking and Healing From Negative Thoughts)

ISBN 978-1-990084-64-5

Legal & Disclaimer

The information contained in this book is not designed to replace or take the place of any form of medicine or professional medical advice. The information in this book has been provided for educational and entertainment purposes only.

The information contained in this book has been compiled from sources deemed reliable, and it is accurate to the best of the Author's knowledge; however, the Author cannot guarantee its accuracy and validity and cannot be held liable for any errors or omissions. Changes are periodically made to this book. You must consult your doctor or get professional medical advice before using any of the suggested remedies, techniques, or information in this book.

Upon using the information contained in this book, you agree to hold harmless the Author from and against any damages, costs, and expenses, including any legal fees potentially resulting from the application of any of the information provided by this guide. This disclaimer applies to any damages or injury caused by the use and application, whether directly or indirectly, of any advice or information presented, whether for breach of contract, tort, negligence, personal injury, criminal intent, or under any other cause of action.

You agree to accept all risks of using the information presented inside this book. You need to consult a professional medical practitioner in order to ensure you are both able and healthy enough to participate in this program.

Table of Contents

Introduction

The following chapters will discuss the different approaches that will help you stop overthinking, procrastinating so that you can spend your time in a much more productive way.

There are plenty of books on this subject on the market, thanks again for choosing this one! Every effort was made to ensure it is full of as much useful information as possible, please enjoy!

Chapter 1: What Is Overthinking?

Overthinking is one of the most common reactions that we tend to have as individuals. Often, we mull over things that have happened, or we believe are going to happen. Of course, it is a valuable skill to have, to reflect and think about the things that have occurred in our lives.

However, it is one thing to reflect with the purpose of learning and growing from the past, and it is another completely different thing to constantly go over and over painful situations that we can't do much about.

Then, there is the dreaded future. When you overthink the future, you are often invaded by thoughts of what could be, or what might not be. You might find yourself constantly concerned about events that, upon rational examination, are unlikely to happen. Yet, your mind is overly active, worried about grave consequences.

In the present, overthinking might take the form of waiting too long to make a decision. You might find yourself being hesitant about what to do, or what to say. Then, before you know it, your opportunity has passed, and you are left with nothing but regret about having missed an opportunity due to your inability to act.

For example, you have been offered the job of your dreams, but it requires you to move to a new city. Naturally, you are inclined to do your homework and conduct research on the new city and company. However, you become paralyzed by thoughts about not having enough information on the new job. You are overly concerned about making the wrong move. Then, you think about past situations in which you may a wrong choice. Soon, you are so hesitant to act that you simply cannot work yourself up to saying "yes" or "no". In the end, your inability to act has led the company to pass on you and give the job to someone else.

As a result, thinking things too much, dwelling on the past for too long, or concerning yourself with the future in excess may lead you to miss the wonderful opportunities that life has for you TODAY.

Chapter 2: What Causes Overthinking?

There are many, many causes of overthinking, many catalysts that trigger the bad habits of overthinking which can lead to anxiety and excessive worrying. These are not pleasant emotions, and what can seem like simply being careful and thinking things through can easily turn into something much more serious and damaging.

We've all experienced worry at some point in our lives. I remember when I was a child, my mother would leave the house very early in the morning to go to work at the post office, and I would wake up just as she was walking out the door and feel a desperate need to run out to the front door and catch her so I could say goodbye and "I love you." This didn't last long, but I remember for a few nights I was overcome by the worry that she was going to leave the house and I would never see her again. This is easily attributable to me being a young child but let us think about another example.

You are an adult, and your older brother is flying out to Colorado for a ski trip with his friends. He's just turned 21, and you know that there is going to be a good deal of partying and drinking going on. Now you start worrying about all the things that could happen. What if he gets in an accident driving around an unfamiliar area? Would he be tempted to drink and drive? What if he falls while skiing and breaks a leg or an arm? What if he runs into a tree and has a concussion and he go to a hospital and I don't know about it because he doesn't have his phone and...and...and...

Okay, so this is an extreme case of acute worry, but I'm sure you know what I'm talking about and have experienced something similar concerning a loved one. To throw a wrench in the works, let's say you just watched a video on Facebook where someone ran right into a tree while skiing a few days ago. Now you have this mental image to feed those worries running through your mind like a broken record. Perhaps you saw a story about a car accident in Colorado caused by bad weather, and now you have that worry going through your mind.

An occasional bout of worry is perfectly normal, but when a person's life becomes plagued by constant worry about things that could happen without a good reason or basis, that person may be suffering from anxiety. There are different forms of anxiety, but two of the most common forms are social and generalized.

We may think of anxiety as a chronic form of overthinking, and many people experience such intense anxiety that they choose to take medication to assuage this feeling. Generalized anxiety applies to everyday experiences which most people get through without trouble. Some people describe the feeling as a "fear of everything." Generalized anxiety affects day-to-day life and manifests as intense worry and fear of things like leaving the house, going to the grocery store, your loved ones' health, what will happen in the world, possibility of war, whether you are eating right, whether you might be sick with serious disease and not know it. Some people suffer from a specific phobia, but generalized anxiety tends to react to many different things at once and can become overwhelming.

You may have experienced some form of anxiety while you began to recognize the habit of overthinking. The first step to address overthinking is to figure out the causes that are specific to you. There are many causes to explore and you will learn as we discuss several of them, even if they don't all apply to you. Hopefully, as you read through this list, you will be able to pinpoint which factors may be playing the biggest role in your overthinking.

Social Expectation

Living and working in the world today is more demanding and challenging than ever before. Yes, we have the modern conveniences that make life more comfortable and convenient, but we also must contend with the structure of social life and the expectation that we follow a timeline that follows something like this: school, more school, entry-level career, climb the ladder, senior-level career, retirement.

For a long time, this was the norm for people living in countries of economic power. But a lot has been shifting over the course of the last few decades, and at an exponentially increasing rate. Finding a job in a lucrative career that will be enjoyable and satisfying for thirty or more years is not so simple anymore. The competition has grown right alongside the earth's population and the staggering advancement of technology. Many of the jobs readily available to our parents no longer exist, and nowadays, you would get a strange look for physically walking into a business and asking for an employment application instead of applying online. If you do manage to get that dream job right out of high school or college, then the real trial by fire begins. We could talk office politics, competition, and rivalry all day, but for right now, let's focus on some of the core triggers for overthinking in two of life's most influential domains: work and school.

We've started to discuss the challenge of finding gainful employment as a young adult in the modern age, so let's continue exploring where overthinking may come into play here.

Following the effect of globalization, the world is now overrun with advertisement and marketing schemes. From the very beginning of your career, you've been told that you will have to compete with many other candidates, many of whom may be more qualified than you. The interview process challenges candidates to make a compelling argument for why they should stand out above all the rest. You may practice in front of a mirror at home or think about all the possible questions that may come up. It is here when you may start thinking about how you measure up next to others in your field. You've just graduated from college with a degree and, at the time, you felt like you were on top of the world with a million different prospects awaiting you (best case scenario, of course). Fast forward a few months, and you start to realize that the job market is a tad more competitive than you thought, and you haven't proven yourself to be a shoo-in to some of your dream companies who have already passed on you. Many young adults in the millennial generation can attest to the challenges of having graduated during a recession in the US and having trouble finding any reasonable employment at all, let alone a prestigious start to a career in their fields.

The pressure of the social expectation that you can and will find a great job if you are smart and work hard enough becomes a great burden if and when things don't work out the way you'd imagined them throughout your time in school. At this point, you may begin to wonder if it is some fault or deficiency within yourself keeping you from your dreams.

The truth is, there are countless factors at play when it comes to finding or landing your "dream job," and sometimes, hard work and a positive attitude are just not enough, despite what your parents or teachers told you. This is why many young adults begin the cycle of overthinking that is dominated by questions of self-worth and adequacy. **If society says I'm supposed to be here or there at this point in my life, that means I've failed and there is something wrong with me.**

Once this conviction takes root, it is very hard to ignore the myriad images, slogans, and advertisements all around us which display the ideal professional man or woman in their nice corner offices, dressed in the latest fashions, sharing how they've made it this far because they work for this or that company, attended this or that school, bought this or that car, bought a house in this or that city, etc. This is when you may start to compare yourself to the success of others, which simply adds to the merry-go-round in your mind that feeds a feeling of inadequacy and low self-esteem.

But now let's say you've landed a decent job. It's not your dream job, but it may be a good start for you and your career. Now it's time to prove yourself. You immediately look around at your coworkers, boss, and peers to assess where you are on the ladder and how you measure up to your competition. Depending on the type of personalities surrounding you, you may feel a lot of pressure to do well and grow within the company. Society teaches us that being the best is the only way to grow and climb within your company, so professional life instantly turns into a competition. This pressure may manifest itself as overthinking every day as you constantly analyze how well you do your job. This is not a bad thing in and of itself—everyone wants to be good at their jobs. A problem arises when we begin obsessively comparing ourselves to others, and when the job is no longer an environment of several likeminded people working to build a better company, but a cutthroat competition to the top.

Once you've managed to break into the top echelons of business society, the competition turns toward other companies in your field—overtaking their market, putting others out of business, etc. And we've all heard the saying, the more you gain, the more you have to lose. This opens up a whole new avenue of worry and overthinking as you assess how far you may fall if you make a mistake or fall off the ladder!

Is this you? Do you experience constant worry about where you are professionally? Maybe you are underemployed and feel embarrassed, like you haven't gone far enough in life as you compare yourself to others. This may be one of the most common triggers for overthinking, but now it's time to move backward in time to examine how social expectation first takes root in our minds as kids. Let's take a look at social expectation in school.

As kids, most of us aren't thinking seriously about what happens after school. We may have some far-fetched dreams swirling in our brains, but mostly we just want to know what mom packed for lunch today and if that big kid is going to knock us off the swing at recess again today. (Hopefully not, but you get the idea.)

As we grow older and enter the realms of middle school and high school, social pressure and expectation become more central to our lives in an immediate sense. We may be thinking of our future careers from a distance, but most of us are preoccupied with whether or not people like us at school, how popular we are, whether or not we'll get a date for the dance, etc. Much of the social pressure at this age centers around physical appearance and either academic or competitive achievement. Sadly, most girls around this age start to become overly concerned about their physical appearance and may even begin to equate this with their self-worth. The trigger for overthinking has begun as these women look around at the beautiful women in social media and in magazines, and begin comparing themselves to those unattainable ideals. Similarly, young boys may have a role model in sports or even a father figure who has become very successful in their professional fields and begin comparing themselves as men, equating success in competitive sports or popularity or academics with their self-worth.

The pressure only gets stronger as we enter college, if that is your path. Balancing social life with academic life is a struggle that many lose, resulting in a student dropping out of college. Remaining focused and achieving good grades and that long-awaited bachelor's degree grants passage into the realm of professional work, where a whole new world of social pressure and expectation awaits.

As you can see, much of our overthinking may very well stem primarily from a distorted perception of ourselves in relationship to others in our professional or social environments. This pressure begins early in life and continues as we are constantly bombarded with images and messages in the media dictating what success should look and feel like.

Let's take a look at some more possible triggers for overthinking.

Relationships

Depending on your age, overthinking in romantic relationships can range from things like, "Does she like me?" to "I just know he's coming home late from work all the time because he's having an affair."

Much of the overthinking that occurs in the minds of people in relationships turns to emotionally painful sources of such feelings as jealousy and low self-esteem. Just as we are bombarded with images of "success" in the media, we are also bombarded with what it should look like to be in a perfect relationship. A young girl who obsesses over her looks in high school may later struggle in a relationship because she perceives other beautiful women as constant threats. Young boys who worry about making money may later struggle in a relationship because he thinks making money and working are more important than quality time spent with a partner.

Overthinking in relationships can cause a lot of problems, and many of them can be quite emotionally draining. When the thoughts taking over one's mind begin to cloud reality, you have the beginning of a self-destructive cycle of negative emotions and perceptions. Outside influences have a way of wheedling themselves into our minds and we begin comparing our relationships to those we see around us, on Facebook, or in other media sources. This is a mistake because every person and relationship is unique—there is no one-size-fits-all system for how a perfect relationship should work. You know you are overthinking when you get mad at your partner because he or she doesn't look at you the same way some famous celebrity looks at his or her partner. Comparing your romantic life to that of others is a great way to miss out on what makes yours special. I'm not saying you should ignore problems in your relationship. I'm saying you shouldn't try to compare those problems with others' problems as a way to solve them.

Each of us is unique, and we all deal with emotions and problems in different ways. Different doesn't mean wrong, but in a society that hides the challenges of a relationship behind the façade of a perfect one, people may experience quite the brutal slap in the face once they move past the "honeymoon phase," and begin to realize it's not all roses and stuffing cake in each other's faces. Relationships aren't supposed to be easy and breezy like the couple makes it seem on all those vacation resort commercials. Comparing and overthinking just makes the challenge more difficult—when the real necessity is communication.

Let's look at two more big sources of overthinking. The first is past trauma.

Trauma

Never a fun topic to broach, but a very important one if this is the cause of overthinking. As mentioned before, we've all experienced some degree of worry when it comes to the safety of ourselves or our loved ones. We worry about our children and their safety, about our spouses, and our aging parents' health, etc. The problem arises when these worries become an ever-present source of stress and anxiety—when the overthinking becomes chronic.

Many adults are affected for the rest of their lives after experiencing some kind of trauma. Many times, the death of a parent can lead to lifelong mindsets and perspectives that can hinder a person's openness and ability to move past painful emotions. Abuse as a child is a serious threat to a person's mental wellbeing and usually needs to be addressed throughout the person's life through treatments such as therapy. When a trauma occurs, it takes ahold of the mind in a way that is very difficult to forget or move past. As a result, the individual may overthink in terms of comparing or viewing other events throughout her life through the lens of that trauma. For example, abuse of a child by an older male may distort a person's ability to deal with men in the future without feeling things like fear, hatred, or aggression. These reactions encompass a much greater threat to overall wellbeing. Many adults manage to compartmentalize as we talked about earlier, or else completely forget or ignore the trauma until it crops up unexpectedly later in life. This is an example of what we call "thought suppression." Sometimes, things are too painful to face, but many believe that the lifelong struggle to contain such pain will only lead to roadblocks in the progress of a person's life. In other words, eventually, the pain must be addressed.

On the level of overthinking, past trauma introduces thoughts and feelings about future events that have no bearing on the present. The fact that you were in a car accident and sustained horrific injuries as a teenager does not mean that every time you get in a car for the rest of your life, you're probably going to get in another accident, but it **feels** this way. We let the influence and strength of those past emotions and fears seep into the events of our lives, even before they've happened. Overthinking in anticipation of something bad happening is a trademark symptom of chronic overthinking.

Finally, I must mention arguably the most universal influence on overthinking—social media addiction.

Social Media

We are all familiar with the recent rhetoric surrounding how everyone is getting addicted to social media. Many of us can't go more than an hour without checking Facebook or our Twitter feeds to see what's new and who liked our latest posts, etc. What you may not realize is that addiction to social media is a powerful source of overthinking. We've discussed such habits as comparing ourselves to others throughout our lives. One of the easiest ways to cultivate this habit is through social media.

When we look at a friend's Facebook page, odds are, we are seeing the pretty, superficially imposed perfect life that they want us and others on the internet to see. We see pictures of people that seem like they are off-the-cuff. But most people take a lot of time preparing their selfies, positioning themselves just right. Many women put on makeup then mess around with the filters until they present the most ideal versions of themselves, they can imagine. You don't see the challenges and stress in that person's life, you just see what they want you to see. This can lead to many of us, once again, comparing our lives to the lives of others who seem prettier, more successful, happier, richer, etc. Those negative feelings like jealousy and self-doubt creep up on us again, just like they did when we were younger and comparing ourselves to the prom queen or the football captain.

All of these thoughts build up over time, and eventually, they may take control, leading to a negative and self-destructive habit of overthinking.

Now that we've pinpointed some of the major triggers for overthinking, let's take a look at the phenomena that all that internet surfing and Facebook scrolling contribute to—information overload.

Chapter 3: Anxiety Disorders

While anxiety is not anything evil I'm itself or anything strange, anxiety disorder is a more serious condition- a health condition that usually requires quick medical attention.

So this chapter will deviate a bit and discuss the term anxiety disorder. This is to help people who might be suffering a disorder or the other. To help them understand their condition and seek help. It will be wicked to, through this book, motivate an anxiety disorder patient to start fighting worries on her own, especially an acute disorder. Any effort will be frustrating and worse off and might not yield desiring results. So the tips enlisted in this book are to the end that an anxious person will begin to live a life devoid of unnecessary worries and anxiety. But then the book still has something for people who have disorders. This chapter has been dedicated to them, to understand themselves more, and take proper measures.

Anxiety Disorder is a term that explains different species of conditions that arise from excessive worrying. The symptoms may vary across persons, based on body type. So, it is the case that while one person's anxiety attack occurs without prior notification or symptom others might have symptoms. One's symptom might be him getting cold feet at the thought of meeting people at a party. Someone else may fret over driving. Yet for another, it could be another may live in a constant state of tension, worrying about anything and everything. Now, these are different manifestations of Anxiety disorder, but despite the various forms that anxiety disorders can take, it all just boils down to it being a serious fear or worry that is out of proportion and is an abnormal reaction to events or occurrences.

If you have ever suffered the sting of an anxiety disorder before, then you will be able to tell how disabling it can get. If you are not careful, it could go as far as changing your course of life, and even debarring you living that life of your dreams.

Now, the first thing you should note is that this is an easy battle because if you decide to fight it, you can almost be so sure that you will win. Anxiety disorders is prominent among top ranking mental health issues, and there have been big successes with its treatment over the years. The essential thing is first to know that you suffer a disorder, then make efforts to understand the basics of your anxiety disorder, and make conscious efforts at reducing the effects you feels, and then regaining your life back.

So do you worry a lot, and are wondering if you have an anxiety disorder? Below, I'll be listing some signs and symptoms that you should look out for, while trying to decipher if you have a disorder or not.

DO I HAVE AN ANXIETY DISORDER?

Now, there are a thousand and one different symptoms that could help you decided your status, so you can know whether or not you have an anxiety disorder. But I'll list seven basic signs that cut across various disorders. If you find yourself exhibiting more than three of these symptoms, then say no more. Possibilities that you have an anxiety disorder is high. Before you go through with the list, understand that it is not a big deal, millions of people are living with a disease in the U.S, so you are not alone. Another thing I would say is that it is easy to confuse Anxiety and Anxiety disorder. So pay attention to my list, do not just run over it, and be sure you understand every symptom before you make your decision. This is so that you won't begin to misdiagnose yourself.

If you are sure that you identify with any three of the underlisted symptoms, then you may be suffering from an anxiety disorder:

Is it the case that you get tensed easily and often, and are always worried and on the edge?

Do you get distracted at work, school or other official engagements as a result of anxiety and worry?

Do you often feel like your fears are unnecessary and irrational but are just locked-in the lifestyle of irrational worries and can't seem to shake it off?

Do you always believe that there is a particular order or orders that things should take if success must be achieved, and then get really disturbed and worried if things don't go that way?

Have you marked out a lot of everyday activities just because they seem to get you anxious.

Do you often have experiences of sudden attacks of intense panic?

Do you sometimes feel unsafe as though danger is lurking somewhere in the corner around you?

If you ticked three of those seven boxes, then that looks like something. Even if you ticked only two, watch it!!

Now, In addition to those symptoms of anxiety disorder that I listed above, here are some more. These ones are emotional symptoms. And they include:

Feelings of apprehension or dread

Always being 'security conscious', suspecting and watching out for signs of danger

Always anticipating the worst

The inability to concentrate

Mostly feeling tensed and jumpy

Easily Irritable

Constant failure to recall things, events, or occurrences.

But anxiety is more than just an emotional feeling. You should understand that it is first a bodily thing, as it is a product of the body's fight-or-flight response to occurrences. So anxiety disorder will involve a wide range of physical symptoms, including:

Incessant heart pounding

Serious headaches

Stomach upset

Dizziness

Frequent urination

Diarrhea

Shortness of breath

Twitches and Muscle tension

Body shaking

Excessive sweating

Insomnia

Sometimes, as a result of the severity of these symptoms, some people mostly misunderstand their symptoms and misconstrue it as a mental problem. In most cases their conditions are not quickly detected by the doctor, they sometimes have to visit many doctors, and visit severally before their condition of anxiety disorder will be detected.

Take note that many people with anxiety disorders also suffer from depression over time. Pundits have it that Anxiety and depression stem from the same biological vulnerability, only that depression is a more severe condition. This should help shed light on the fact that depression and anxiety often go hand-in-hand. So once anxiety disorder is detected, the sufferer must get immediate help.

WHAT CAUSES ANXIETY DISORDERS?

This problem- anxiety may be caused by a mental condition or a physical health. It could be an effect of drugs and drug abuse, or from a combination of these.

So first, when you get to the hospital, the first thing your doctor should attend to is, finding the root cause of the anxiety disorder. Be truthful in answering and be open. Do not hide information away from your doctor. If he can find the cause and trigger factor, then tell. He would most likely be able to determine what variant of disorder it is, so don't refrain. Did I mention that it could be caused by medical conditions too? Yes, it can. States as varied as anemia, asthma attack, infections, drug intoxication or withdrawal, or some heart conditions are just a few examples of medical problems that can be associated with anxiety disorder

Types of Anxiety Disorder

A phobia

Phobia is a term you are familiar with I guess. It is not a strange word, in fact, the majority of us can testify to having one phobia or the other.

Phobia is nothing but the fear of an events, activity, or an object, even persons. This fear is usually unrealistic, unjustifiable, and uncalled for. It is often a grave reaction to a situation that, has little or no danger in itself. There is a long list of phobias that we see around, but an example of common phobias include fear of animals, fear of water like oceans, springs, (very rampant), and fear of people. These exposures may trigger a panic attack. Phobia gets to the extreme when sufferers go as far as totally avoiding the person, situation, or activity that they fear. It is an unpopular fact that the more you avoid your phobia, the stronger it becomes.

Social anxiety disorder

This one is also a common fear. It borders on social acceptance. Some people will instead not even meet people or attend social meet ups for fear of being regarded as being odd, saying or doing the wrong thing, and being embarrassed in public. All of these are just pointers to social anxiety disorder. This disorder can also be called social phobia. Sometimes, some people mistake social anxiety disorder for the case of extreme shyness. But this is not true, especially in severe cases, where social situations are do not appeal anymore and are therefore avoided.

Performance anxiety

Performance anxiety is common among shy people and children. Did I say that, let's assume I didn't and go over it again? Well, performance anxiety, which is also known as stage fright, is common among most individuals. We get scared when we are about to mount a podium and speak, sing, or perform to an audience. It is a normal phenomenon, if still mild and controllable. But once a person begins to behave abnormally at the mention of the need to publicly address people, then it might be a problem.

Performance anxiety is one of the most common types of Anxiety disorder.

Post-traumatic stress disorder (PTSD)

Post-traumatic stress disorder (PTSD) is one form of anxiety disorder. It is really extreme, and it often occurs as an effect of a traumatic or life-threatening event. PTSD can be likened to a panic attack. It can sometimes take up so much time before it lets its sufferer free. It is caused by a person's experience of either death or near-death circumstances. These circumstances can range from fire incidences, floods, earthquakes, shootings, automobile accidents, to wars. Not all traumatic events always include death or near-death instances. Some other traumatic events may be the incidence of serious injury or threat; examples of such trauma includes victimization through physical or sexual abuse, witnessing the violence of another or over-exposure to inappropriate material. This traumatic event then resurfaces over and over again in the sufferer's thoughts and dreams. And when it gets to that point, it is then called post-traumatic stress disorder. Common symptoms include the following:

A pseudo-re-experience of the trauma

Difficulty in concentrating

Difficulty in sleeping at night

Feeling a general sense of depression

Irritability

Doom and gloom

Little or no expectations of a bright future.

hypervigilance

Always getting startled easily

Withdrawal from people

Total avoidance of situations, people, and things that can remind the sufferer of the event.

Symptoms such as chest pain, shortness of breath, palpitations, dizziness, fainting, and weakness generally can all be attributed to anxiety and require evaluation by a doctor.

Separation anxiety disorder

This disorder is common in childhood. You'll see kids often get moody, cry, create scenes, and sometimes stay in solitude because they miss someone they love, or perceive that such a person will leave them soon, either temporarily or permanently. But watch it, it might look normal, but if this anxiety intensifies and gets persistent enough to prevent the kid from making new friends, talking to others, going to, and participating in school or other activities, then the child may have a separation anxiety disorder. This condition is common among, but not restricted to just children. Few adults can be like this, too, when they miss the people they love.

Panic disorder

A panic attack is another significant and dominant disease. It works in a way that its sufferers will have particular sensations of their mind going blank or that they somehow cannot feel themselves as themselves anymore. They get to that point where they think external to themselves. These disorders are separate and intense periods of fear or feelings of doom that it builds up gradually, over a long while, but gets noticeable in a short while. It gets dangerous when the individual experiences it repeatedly, having more panic attacks rather than just one episode. The common symptoms of these panic disorders include stomach upset, palpitations (feeling your heartbeat), dizziness, and shortness of breath.

Note that these symptoms are not particular to just panic attacks; they could be the effects of the excessive consumption of any of the following:

Caffeine

Amphetamines ("speed")

An overactive thyroid

An abnormal heart rhythm

Mitral valve prolapse

Recurrent episodes of panic attacks can be associated with restlessness, constant tiredness, loss of concentration, irritability, muscle tension, and sleep problems.

Generalized anxiety disorder

Those who endure this condition experience numerous worries that are more often on the mind of the sufferer than not. Those worries interfere with the person's ability to sleep; it frequently affects appetite, energy level, concentration, and other aspects of daily functioning.

When to Seek Medical Care for Anxiety

In some cases, anxiety could get better on its own over a while, without medication. It is common for anxiety attacks that do not last for long duration of time, and whose causal factors are known and can be worked upon. There are cases of ones with more extended periods too that go away on their own, but most of the time, we find it difficult knowing when to take salvaging and when to stay hopeful that the situation at hand is not difficult, and would naturally go away. Now, it can be hazardous if treatments do not start in time for an anxiety disorder patient. So, below are some of the right timings to seek medical care for anxiety. You totally should invite your doctor over, if:

The signs and symptoms of the kind of stress that you feel does not go off in time even with the application of homemade remedies to Anxiety. (They will be discussed extensively through out the book)

Once the symptoms are seriously interfering with your mind, and probably already making a mess of your personal, social, or professional life.

If you experience physical abnormals like chest pain, shortness of breath, headaches, palpitations, dizziness, fainting spells, or unexplained weakness.

Yes, this is clear, and I feel you should already know this before now; that if you are depressed and you sometimes get suicidal or homicidal thoughts, then you should see your doctor.

When the signs and symptoms suggest that anxiety may have been present for a prolonged period, maybe for more than a few days, and it is becoming your everyday mood, and is probably getting worse, then you should see a doctor.

If the symptoms you feel are so severe that you believe strongly that medication may be needed. Do not discard the dictation of your intuition. If they are so severe, and probably developed suddenly, then they may be signs of a serious medical illness. The best bet is to get checked by your doctor, so you can tell what exactly it is.

Home Remedies for Anxiety

Before heading straight off to the hospital or seeking external help, one can try some of these tips to help remedy the situation. The following tips are useful for cases of anxiety that are not so serious, For example, anxiety over an upcoming public performance, a final exam, or a pending job interview. Anxiety in such circumstances can be combatted using any of the following methods.

Use your mind

First, employ the power of your mind. You'll have to paint a picture in your mind. See yourself successfully facing and conquering the specific fear that has brought you anxiety.

Open up

Another thing that will be useful will be you opening up to someone. And note that you should not open up to just anybody, but someone whose support you can be sure of. Not someone who will eventually spite you, or talk down on your problem. Generally, talking about your worries face to face with somebody can often make them seem less overwhelming. So, talking with a supportive person can be helpful.

Meditation

Engage your ability to meditate, and do this often, it could be super-efficient in fighting this challenge.

Engaging in recreational activities

Activities like taking a long walk, hanging out with friends, seeing a movie, or just staying in front of the Television, could help out. It although is a temporary solution, but at the moment, it will help in stealing you off the pangs of anxiety.

Taking a long, warm bath

Have you ever just sat in the bath and just relaxed there, or in a pool, just ruminating and letting the water calm your nerves. You really should try it out.

Resting in a dark room

This is another weird method that you can try out. When I was a kid, I loved staying in dark places alone, but over time I often got scolded and forced out of my hiding, and I decided that it was probably a bad thing and that that was probably the reason older folks always forced me out.

But away from me, resting in dark rooms performs magic on you. It kind of numbs your brain and keeps it from running off on too much thought and worries. This way, you are just still and calm.

Deep-breathing exercises

Whenever you breath in deeply for a while and let out the breathe, you send a message to your brain that you are fine and that there is no cause for alarm. Do this as many times as you can remember during the day, and work towards making it a habit. It is a healthy one.

How to Prevent Anxiety Disorders

Anxiety disorders are not some contagious conditions or some conditions that just fall on you. It is highly preventable, although not all of them. But to prevent anxiety, first you have to understand, and not just understand, but also internalize the fact that life is full of ups and down, and full of stress. Once you are able to deal with this fact, then you will now start to build up coping mechanisms with which you will relate with these stresses. Let me intimate you with the fact that it is not as easy as I just said it. Especially in this very busy time in which we live, it is always difficult to track your activities, stress triggers and evaluate your responses and reactions to these stress triggers. But holistically have a joy-informed mindset to life. Understand the principle of forgiveness, letting-go, having little expectations, optimizing peace and finally the principle of contentment. Below are some coping mechanisms that you should develop to be able to effectively tackle all of life's stresses.

Protect your physical well-being with consistent exercises- Exercise is an important part of physical and mental health, healthy eating habits, and adequate rest. All of these will assist in easing your feelings of anxiety and boosting your sense of well-being.

Avoid the excessive ingestion of caffeine and illicit drugs.

Meditation helps, try out meditation

Relaxation exercises

Sign up for a class or just do something totally out of the norm for you. You could as well join an association or club.

Visualization. Visualization helps a great deal.

Try out volunteer jobs.

Make constant visits to the prison, homeless babies homes

If anxiety is making it hard for you to fall asleep, create a routine that will make sleep more appealing to the goal that it can help you catch sleep.

Try to stick to a schedule.

Always make your bed

Use interesting and bright colors to paint your room, or office.

Sleep on a comfortable mattress.

Dare your anxiety triggers

Schedule your worry time.

Stay positive.

Be the boss of your thoughts.

Tame tense muscles. Relax them with simple exercises.

Volunteer to help out in your community. Meet needs.

Look for the patterns with which you get triggered, and the factors that are usually responsible.

If you know the causes of your anxiety, that can help you put your worries into perspective. Next time, you'll be better prepared when it affects you.

Connect with others

Chapter 4: Defining Worry

In a seemingly busy world, it is not a strange thing to feel worried at certain times. Worrying is generally a central feature of an anxiety disorder. Worry can be classified as any fears, ideas, images, feelings, and thoughts, which are naturally cynical, and that occurs as a response to either imagined or real impending problems.

It is very imperative to note that this extensive definition encompasses quite much. It could include stressful thoughts that regard the future of a person, worrying about your current financial situation, or even stressful thoughts that surround an upcoming medical operation. If, by any chance, you imagine something and notice that it is a bother, then the above definition of worry will best suit it.

Worrying can also be perceived as a self-talk activity where we talk to ourselves repeatedly concerning the possible negative or positive events that might take place, and of which we get frightened of at times.

In most cases, we mentally hold self-discussions with ourselves over and over again and think about what would always occur when the event takes place. That makes worrying a kind of vigilance for threat, and also an attempt at mentally fixing problems that have not yet taken place. The word "attempt" is used here since a lasting solution does not always happen. And people still think they might not cope should anything terrible happen to them.

In other words, worrying is another kind of repetitive negative thinking, where we get trapped, locked, caught, and stuck in the negative thoughts about the upcoming bad things. This kind of negative thinking has a snowball-like, spiral, or circular feature to it since the same negative stuff will be rehashed repeatedly in our minds. When that happens, there will always be a problem safely disengaging from some of these negative thoughts. This process of thinking frequently fuels our anxious feelings, and the topic of worrying us will get bigger and bigger.

Essentially, worry is the thinking or cognitive part of anxiety. It is composed up of fearful thoughts about some of the things that

• Are occurring

• Have occurred or

• Could occur

Fearful thoughts could be both negative and intrusive. Worry, to some individuals, is an occasional experience. For other people, worry can be a typical way of thinking or a constant adventure.

As pointed out at the beginning of the e-book, it is not a strange thing to be engulfed in worries at certain times. There are a number of things that you can worry about, such as your family, your business, and a host of other personal problems. Sometimes, though, worry can get out of hand and become a problem that might not end anytime soon. It might interfere with your day-to-day routine and even interfere with your ability to concentrate at your job, and also bar you from getting asleep at night. Worse still, you might find yourself not able to do anything about worry until it takes full control of your life.

According to studies, we all worry about nearly the same bunch of problems. It is, however, the amount of time we spend worrying and the kind of difficulty that we face to disengaging from worry that would tell if our worry is problematic or not.

A number of people think about negative things and worry from time to time, these worrisome sentiments do not last for long for the most part. They either give way to another thought topic popping into mind or may be solved once and for all by a positive problem-solving set of actions. Worry only gets unhelpful when it is consistent and gets so hard to disengage from or control. When such a thing occurs, we will be trapped in our negative thoughts.

Regardless of whether you worry as a result of something internal or external, the first what-if thought will come to your mind and is likely to be accompanied by specific emotional and uncomfortable physical symptoms. These symptoms would include anxious feelings, butterflies, and tension, among others. So far, this happens to all and would be considered just as usual.

The positive perception you have concerning worrying will imply that you respond to the original "what if" thought with more negative thinking and worry. This is because you believe it is a sensible thing to do. Therefore, you grant negative thoughts more attention and time, which then turn them into more worrisome thinking.

When that happens, your attention will be locked on such worrisome thoughts, and it would be so hard to come out of that situation. Your unhelpful attention is either not able to move to a more helpful focus or unaware that it has been caught in worry. It is just like the task that you have at hand, which only fuels your preoccupation with more of your worries.

Difference Between Worry and Anxiety

The terms worry, and anxiety are always used interchangeably, although they are totally different psychological states. Even though both of them are linked to an overall sense of disquiet and concern, how they are experienced is a bit distinct, and so the implications that they have for our psychological and emotional health.

Anxiety is that kind of uneasy apprehension, or a feeling of misfortune, doom, or danger. In clinical terms, anxiety is a response to perceived risk or threat. In most cases, it is produced when a person starts to anticipate future events. It is important to note that there is a difference between anxiety as a feeling and anxiety as a disorder. It is possible to feel anxious and fail to have an anxiety disorder. On the other hand, anxiety can also be a symptom of a number of other psychiatric disorders, as well.

Anxiety is always prompted by fear, which is a warning system that is created into our bodies as a natural reaction to danger. In the presence of real danger, it is just okay to feel fear. However, when fear goes beyond real danger and starts to linger in our minds, then that becomes worry or anxiety. It is always prompted by feelings and uncertainty that are out of control, a reality that we all have to handle in the best manner.

As a psychiatric disorder, anxiety relates to confronting a feared situation or an object. It is prolonged and excessive and always includes worry. It also tends to interfere with day-to-day life. Worry, on the other hand, is the mental part of anxiety. It has to do with anxious thoughts such as "What If..."

Your thoughts will always influence your behavior and feelings. Therefore, getting control of worried thoughts is one of the essential steps in living a stress-free life.

Main Differences between Anxiety and Worry

We always experience anxiety in our bodies and worry in our heads. Worry appears to be focused on the thoughts that we have in our heads, while anxiety is more visceral. This is due to the fact that we feel it our bodies.

While anxiety is more diffuse, worry tends to be very specific. We usually worry about things such as getting to the airport on time but feel anxious about a planned journey. Travelling, when compared to getting to the airport on time, is a more general and vaguer concern.

Anxiety includes mental imagery and verbal thoughts, while worry is verbally focused. This kind of difference is very vital since emotional, mental images like those connected with anxiety tend to provoke away much higher cardiovascular response than the irrational verbal thoughts. This is also another reason why anxiety is always experienced throughout the entire body.

Worry always activates problem-solving while worry does not. Worry can make us start thinking about strategies and solutions for handling a particular situation. Anxiety can be compared to a hamster wheel that has the main aim of ensuring that we spin around but does not lead to any productive solutions. As a matter of fact, the diffuse nature of anxiety makes it way less amenable to the whole issue of problem-solving.

While anxiety can create serious emotional distress, worry tends to create mild emotional distress. It is important to note that anxiety is way much more powerful and can, therefore, lead to problematic and disruptive psychological state as compared to worry.

Worry is brought about by more realistic concerns as compared to anxiety. It would be called worry when you are really stressed about getting losing your job if you did averagely low on your project. But if you are concerned about getting fired since your boss failed to ask about the piano recital of your child, then you are just anxious.

Worry can be controlled, while anxiety is less controllable. We can greatly diminish worry through problem-solving and weighing some of the ways of dealing with it. However, there is much less control than we have over our anxiety since it is much harder to talk ourselves out of.

Worry is a temporary state. Anxiety will linger on for a very long time. Once we have solved the issue that is responsible for our worry, our worry will diminish and fade away. Anxiety, on the other hand, can linger for extended periods of time and even jump from a single focus to the other.

Worry does not affect our personal and professional function, but anxiety does. Nobody can take a sick day to worry if their teenager will perform well in their assessment tests. However, we can be so restless as a result of the anxiety. Anxiety will even make us unable to concentrate and yet feel so tired to also continue with our daily activities.

Worry is a normative state of psychology, while anxiety is not. There are certain durations and intensities where anxiety is considered a real mental disorder, one that needs medication or psychological treatment.

Why the Difference Between Anxiety and Worry Matters?

In regular daily conversations, anxiety, and worry tend to be used so interchangeably. When a person says he's very anxious about an upcoming test, he implies that he is just worried. However, when it comes to psychology, anxiety, and worry are two different things. One is actually more severe than the other one.

Anxiety is general; worry is exact - With worry, we can tell what is giving us sleepless nights. But when it comes to anxiety, things are more vague and widespread. At times anxiety can be so general to a point where we even don't know what is causing it at all. All you know is that you are feeling under threat, agitated, and tense.

Anxiety is irrational; worry makes sense – Anxiety makes sense in very rare cases outside our thoughts. But when it does, it tends to so dramatic.

Anxiety is everywhere, while worry is escapable and limited – Each time we worry, it tends to be in a given area of life. Anxiety, on the other hand, tends to leak into all the regions.

Anxiety is physical, while worry is mental and verbal – It is important to note that worry is thought-based. It can surely keep us thinking all night, but it is not something we can physically feel. Apart from affecting our sleep, anxiety can also cause us a number of physical symptoms. They include jaw clenching, teeth grinding, dry mouth, and sweating. Others are a racing heart, lightheadedness, dizziness, and an upset stomach.

Anxiety can significantly affect your functioning – Worry can be very annoying, but it can't stop you from your daily life. You will still have an opportunity to go on with your work, have a social life, and perform better. On the other hand, anxiety will significantly change your ability to be effective in your work. You might notice that your performance in school starts going down. In this case, all your energy will be taken by your anxious thoughts without your knowledge.

Both anxiety and worry are worth talking to a counselor. However, anxiety is much out of control and pervasive as compare to worry. As time moves by, anxiety can develop into anxiety disorders, panic attacks, severe depression, and anxiety disorders. All of these can significantly affect your ability to function in the best manner. It is very imperative to get help for any anxiety-related problem as quick as possible. It is easier to treat general anxiety than major depression or an anxiety disorder.

Chapter 5: Identifying Core Values

What Are Core Values?

Core values are thoughts, routines, rituals, and manners that you were taught to follow. They are ideals and customs observed by family, friends, and leaders taught to you as you grew up. They are beliefs also called personal values that you usually share in common with people in your social circle.

Core values help guide people in how they live their lives, interact with others, and guide our decision making. Core values are not strategies or operating practices. They are not part of competencies or cultural norms. They don't change with the market, administrative, or political changes, and are not used individually.

Core values guide us in personal relationships, teaching others, conducting business, and in decision making. They clarify who we are and for what we stand. They can help explain why we conduct business the way we do and are a platform for our businesses.

These often differ from culture to culture, family to family, and person to person. A guide will be provided for you, but you are encouraged to enhance and change the example to include your core values. There is a list of core value words in chapter 8 that can help you fill out your chart.

Many businesses and government departments craft core value statements and mission statements to guide employees. They are meant to instill a strong sense of purpose and standards for which they strive to achieve.

For example, the U.S. Air Force core values are **integrity first, service before self, and excellence in all we do**. You have a clear idea of what is expected from your work with the U.S. Air Force when you read this. It is a commitment that each Airman makes when he joins the force.

~ Core Values help those who join us to understand right from the outset what's expected of them. Equally important, they provide all of us, from [the rank of] Airman to four-start general, with a touchstone -- a guide in our own conscience -- to remind us of what we expect from ourselves. We have wonderful people in the Air Force. But we aren't perfect. Frequent reflection on the core values helps each of us refocus on the person we want to be and the example we want to set. ~

- General Michael E. Ryan, Chief of Staff, United States Air Force (CSAF), 1997-2001.

To determine where your concerns might lie, let's try another exercise. You want to be in a calm, clear state of mind for this exercise. Phone off, family in bed, dog walked. Take a few deep breaths and clear your mind.

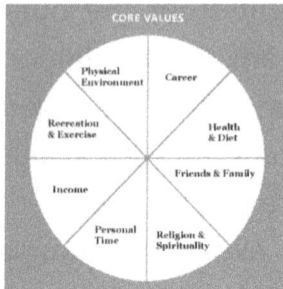

Grab your pad and pen and create a pie chart with as many slices as you need. I have selected eight areas with values familiar to the average American. You may need to add or change some of the headings to fit your life.

You may need to sub-divide some of these slices because I am going to ask you to rate your satisfaction on a scale of 1 to 10 where 1 is totally unsatisfied and 10 is totally satisfied. You might be happy with one aspect of your career but wish to improve upon other areas.

Now let's look at some sub-categories of these slices.

Physical Environment at work. Think of the surroundings in which you work, is the atmosphere uplifting? Are your surroundings loud or quiet, chaotic or controlled, bland or bright, energy-draining or uplifting? Do you feel safe or exposed, is there anything living around you (fish tank, plants, terrariums)?

There may not be too much you can control about work, cubicles and beige paint being what they are. But is your own area clear of clutter and neat with a few items that (if allowed) help create a positive mood to make the most out of your workday?

Now, I realize if you are a K-3 teacher, there are some chaos, loud noises, and draining energy that comes with the job. However, is it controlled chaos, and happy singing at the top of their lungs?

How satisfied are you with your work environment on a scale of 1-10?

Physical Environment at home. You may be limited to what you can do if you are renting, have roommates, or family who's taste differ from yours. But think about your work and play spaces in the home, inside and out. Do you like them? If not, what would you like to change? Think about your ideal living environment.

How satisfied are you with your home environment on a scale of 1-10?

Career. Is your career moving along at the pace you expected or wanted? Are you happy with your projects, clients, co-workers, and company reputation?

How satisfied are you with your career on a scale of 1-10?

Health & Diet. Are you in good health? Are you carrying extra weight or stress? How are your blood pressure and blood sugar? Do you smoke? Do you drink?

How satisfied are you with your health & diet on a scale of 1 to 10?

Family & Friends. Is there anything you would like to change about your relationship with your family? Too much scheduled a time and not enough quality time? Empty nest syndrome? Stressed about someone else's situation? Lack of input into family get-togethers? Holiday nightmares?

How satisfied are you with your family and friends' relationships on a scale of 1 to 10?

Religion & Spirituality. Are you spending enough time feeding your inner spirit? This could be services, volunteer work, or more time in nature.

How satisfied are you with your religious and spiritual experience on a scale of 1 to 10?

Personal Time. Do you get to take a nap once in a while? Spend time with friends, perhaps without spouse or family? There should be some time during the week that isn't dictated by work or others.

How satisfied are you with your amount of personal time on a scale of 1 to 10?

Income. Are you satisfied with the amount of income you have available?

Are you able to save a set percentage of your pay? You may not be where you want to be financially, but are you on track with a plan to accomplish your financial goals?

How satisfied are you with your financial goals and savings on a scale of 1 to 10?

Recreation & Exercise. For most people, there is not a significant amount of time available for recreation or exercise, so we skip it. This is not a slice to put on the back burner. The old saying: "The more you do, the more you want to do" is very true.

How satisfied are you with your time for exercise and recreation on a scale of 1 to 10?

Let's see what some answers might look like. For this example, I'm using a 37-year-old mother of two, divorced for eight months. She has a career and shares custody of the children with her ex-husband:

Physical Environment - Work (7) - not much we can change, but it is a quiet work environment, with working equipment and up-to-date software.

Physical Environment - Home (5) - I can't seem to keep up with everything. I'm doing well to get the clothes washed and folded, and dinner cleaned up. The main rooms get vacuumed regularly, but the other rooms only once or twice a month. And I never have time for yard work, since the divorce. I can't even think about painting or replacing anything right now while the kids are still in grade school.

Career - (8) - I'm lucky to get to work in my field of choice, and it is a good company for working mothers.

Health & Diet - (5) - Doc says I'm 40 lbs. overweight. I think I eat well, just too much.

Friends & Family - Friends (8) - I have several circles of friends: parents from the children's school/events, some from college, and some from work. Although, again, since the divorce, my time has been limited and I don't see them very often. Maybe it used to be an eight.

Friends & Family - Family (6) - Quite a bit of our family is still in this area, and when I first started dating seriously and graduated from college, I had to set some boundaries for my own free time. Maybe that number should be higher; I'm actually seeing more of both sides since the divorce.

Religion & Spirituality - (8) - for both. I keep the kids close to nature and their father and his family shares their religion.

Personal Time - (2) - The only time I have to myself is getting ready for bed, sleeping and getting up in the morning.

Income - (8) - It's tighter now that we have two households, but we are okay.

Recreation & Exercise - (5) - Again, time is tight with all of the children's events. I don't have much time for my exercise - those are some of the friends I've been missing. I haven't even thought about vacation, given all the changes.

As you have time, change the chart to suit your life and think about your answers. Fill out this exercise and set this chart aside in your work folder. We will be using this later when creating your action plan.

How Do You Worry?

~ Worrying is carrying tomorrow's load with today's strength - carrying two days at once. It is moving into tomorrow ahead of time. Worrying doesn't empty tomorrow of its sorrow, it empties today of its strength. ~

- Corrie Ten Boom

As we have already noted, everybody worries. But you may have noticed that some people handle worries better than others. We've all seen the person who always seems to be concerned about the problems of everyone they meet. Then there are those who seem to never be worried, never show that emotion. There are different types of worrying.

Time-sensitive catastrophic: If an event doesn't happen in the time specified, he or she begins to fret. The longer the delay, the more time and energy this person spends worrying. Their worries are overblown and center around the worst-case scenario. For this worrier, life can seem impossible to manage.

My grandmother was one of these. If your plane was supposed to land at 5:30 and you were expected home by 6:30 - if you were not in the house by 6:31 she started worrying. By 7:00 she wanted us to call the hospital to check for accident victims, it was exhausting for everyone.

Victim: Everything is out of this person's control. They have no power and no one understands. They don't trust people, feel taken advantage of and cheated or abused.

Avoidant: With low self-esteem, this worrier is a people-pleaser and worries about not being good enough. There are trust issues and this person seeks reassurance from others.

Compulsive: This person worries about their work and productivity keeping tight schedules. They are overly devoted to work and set very high standards for themselves and others.

Obsessive: This person is triggered by anything that goes wrong or not according to plan, for anyone in their direct vicinity. This type of worrier expends way too much time and energy on things he or she cannot control. It's a full-time occupation for this person. They put every situation under a microscope and repeat all outcomes in their head. You know this person, if something happens on the news, in the office, or even to a celebrity they worry over it all day long. It affects their work, and their co-workers.

Controlled: Yes, something bad may have happened but there is nothing they can do about the situation. They carry on with their day even with the worry.

Fortunately, we all also know some of these people and should follow their example. They don't let worries consume them to the point they can think of nothing else.

Histrionic: The queen bee, people are attracted to this person's charisma and imagination. Constantly attracting drama to keep people interested in their calling card. They don't want to be out of the spotlight.

Dependent: This worrier is worried about abandonment and shows devotion and loyalty to the point of being clingy and needy in relationships. He or she will do anything to keep connected to friend or lover.

Narcissistic: This person believes that he or she deserves special attention. They crave admiration and worry about keeping up the appearance of perfection. Status and position are everything and they worry constantly about others finding chinks in their armor.

Social: This worrier appears worry-free, but for all their fun and charm, is afraid their risk-taking and excitement will come with a price. He or she is constantly worried about the trouble that might catch up. With rule-breaking and sometimes hurting other people in the process of having a good time, will this time be their last?

Passive-Aggressive: This person worries about all the things that could go wrong, or that he or she is not good enough, or fret about how much it's probably going to cost, instead of just getting the job done. Anticipation is usually worse than reality. They can worry about confrontation and speaking their truth to others. They resist their wishes and those of others through procrastination, stubbornness or feigning forgetfulness.

At the top of a new page, make a note as to what type of worrier you might be. Underneath your worry type, list what it is you worry about during your day. Chapter

8 has a list of topics if you need some help getting started.

Type of Worrier: Passive-Aggressive Worrier	Over-thinking Loop	Efficiency Problem	Sharing Opportunity	Possible Solutions
Unexpected bills	x			List - Payment schedule/credit card
Renter is not paying		x		Send info to Eviction Lawyer - alert handyman for cleanup - fine

				propert y mgmt. group.
Not good enough for a dance performa nce	x			practice
Lose weight for costumes	x			what are you eating
Practice steps 3 times a day		x		scheduli ng - can't find notes org
Organize hobby/wo rk/home	x			List and schedul e
Dogs need bath			x	teach oldest to bath

				small dogs
The kitchen sink is always full of dirty dishes			x	end of meal routine - 3 weeks
House needs a thorough cleaning	x			family meeting - ask for help
Kids aren't using hamper for dirty clothes			x	family meeting - other routines
Wet towels in the hamper			x	family meeting - tired of repeating myself
Work out children's	x			Make an agenda

savings account with Ex				similar to a work meeting - stick to it.
Repairs on kitchen	x			List - order

Control

~ Be not angry that you cannot make others as you wish them to be since you cannot make yourself as you wish to be ~

- Thomas a Kempis, The Imitation of Christ

Analysis Loop

Do you find that you can remember certain conversations word for word? You turn them over and over in your head analyzing what was discussed. Why do you think those particular discussions stuck in your head? Let's see if we can figure out what it was about the topic that upset you so.

On a new page write the title Analysis Loop, make a left-hand column with the following rows: Who, What, Outcome, Feelings, and Desired Outcome. If you don't have conversation churning currently and can't remember a recent conversation, read through this information and come back to the exercise when you need it.

In the example below, the frustrated party is a middle manager with new purchasing software to install across the entire company. Every department for every company will be required to enter supply orders into a central database at Corporate so that the company may leverage purchasing power. Corporate owns 21 companies across the US.

	Analysis Loop - Why are you looping through this particular discussion?
Who:	Executive Committee (all department directors for your

	company)
What:	The production department has a project it wants to implement prior to your purchasing project. Problem: Corporate has required all companies to be up and running in four months. The production project is going to eat up for two months, leaving you only two months to implement.
Outcome:	Production is granted a go for their project (which requires work from your people to help with software install and some training).
Feelings:	ineffective, unsupported, taken for granted, anger
Desired Outcome:	Greenlight to complete the purchasing project prior to starting productions project.

Imagine how this manager must feel. He went into a meeting with the senior members of the company expecting to get the go over the production project due to the deadline. Instead, the exact opposite happens. Now, some might take that as a vote of confidence in the technology department to get the job done in half the time. But in the particular case, the manager felt he needed the full four-month timeline for the project.

Now he must work through his disappointment and not let it show. Handle the stress of two projects one in half the installation time he'd been given originally. Never mind the daily obstacles that every tech department faces.

Reasons & Meaning

This next example is more of an emotional loop. The sensation of Hear Me Now! You want someone to agree with your vision. Or you want very desperately to have an **adventure** with some friends or a friend, but it is not going to happen. The truth is that you can't force, orchestrate, or recreate good times. You can't make people like you or always sway their opinion.

	Analysis Loop - Why are you looping through this particular discussion?
Who:	Running buddy
What:	10 K fundraiser over in a different county (as opposed to doing the same one you did last year in your county). You've repeatedly let running buddy pick races over some you wanted to do and have been supportive.
Outcome:	Running buddy has no interest, wants to do the same races as last year.
Feelings:	Frustration, anger, hurt, disappointment, disinterest
Desired Outcome:	A resounding 'Yes, let's do something new!'

Get up your brave and sign up for that other race. You might meet new friends.

Run into old friends at the race you hadn't thought of asking.

Chapter 6: How To Gain Total Control

Over Fear And Anxiety?

Dread and anxiety come side by side. They are, be that as it may, controllable however the way to do so isn't as simple. Panic, trepidation, and stress are what make the impacts of dread and anxiety. Knowing the reason that triggers dread and anxiety in an individual can be a decent answer for taking care of the issues and controlling assaults of dread and anxiety.

Anxiety and dread obviously make an emergency in a man's life. It can influence one's ability to fill in his mind-set which can prompt relationship issues with other people. It is thus a significant worry for everyone to see how dread and anxiety attempts to demolish their lives. Overseeing anxiety, controlling apprehension, and in the end defeating trepidation and anxiety is a simple expression to state, however is much progressively hard to place without hesitation.

Dread and anxiety jump out at the two kids and grown-ups. There are a few different ways on the most proficient method to beat these issues adequately even without spending a great amount of time searching for costly books that claim to have the solution to your inquiries.

So what precisely are the things that should have been finished?

In the first place, we have to pinpoint why and when the issue is well on the way to happen. Dread and anxiety assaults trigger now and again when we are generally helpless. In a circumstance when we feel apprehensive and restless, our inclination is well on the way to be uneasy and scared, which makes us generally an excellent objective for dread and anxiety.

At the point when this circumstance happens, our body does not react regularly and we fundamentally can't control our sentiments which results in the issue. This torment, pressure and stress cooperate, which legitimately assaults our sensory system making it powerless and unfit to work appropriately and the outcome - dread and anxiety.

Clearing the psyche is the probably ideal approache to counteract anxiety assaults. Making a rundown of the things that make you stressed or experience dread is one approach to do this. This can enable you to facilitate your psyche and discharge the negative things that are thundering in your mind.

At the point when the main alternative comes up short, and you feel that a dread or anxiety assault is going to happen, you have one more line of guard against this circumstance occurring. Center and grab quiet is the subsequent arrangement.

Quiet yourself by occupying your thoughtfulness regarding the things that can make either your psyche or your body occupied. Normally things that are not exhausting to do are the best consideration diverters. Changing your propensities can likewise work. Keeping away from forlorn spots or going someplace with other individuals is another great answer to the issue.

HOW TO OVERCOME FEAR AND ANXIETY

Starting your eye exercise program may appear to be a troublesome and overwhelming undertaking. Be that as it may, from a positive perspective, it doesn't need to be a difficult endeavor. With regards to change, dread and anxiety are obstacles that fill in as hindrances, keeping us from accomplishing our objectives. In the event that you have been familiar with wearing your glasses or contacts for quite a while, it's reasonable that this takeoff from customary techniques for vision improvement would be seen with some worry and anxiety, Due to a dread of the obscure. In this way, if dread and anxiety are keeping you away from starting your vision improvement program, here are a few hints that tell you the best way to defeat dread and anxiety.

The dread of being disparaged for picking a characteristic vision improvement program, a way less went in the field of vision improvement, may make you become somewhat fearful. You might be stressed or worried that your loved ones may scorn you or even blame you for being insane for performing eye works out. Transform this negative into a positive. Utilize this negative circumstance furthering your potential benefit. Become so resolved to prevail at your vision improvement objectives that it causes your companions and relatives to respect your commitment and endurance to the program. As you keep on driving forward with the methods, they will build up regard for you. As your common vision keeps on improving significantly, your companions will see the positive outcomes: decreased reliance on glasses and more prominent visual autonomy.

Their frame of mind to you will be increasingly positive, and they may consider doing what you are doing. Another option is to pick a private practice zone where you can play out the strategies in the security of your own home free of diversions.

Think about dread as an exercise that once learned, would prompt something positive and fulfilling; something that encourages you to develop throughout everyday life. Regularly, we think little of our capacities to achieve undertakings in life that appear to be overwhelming from outward appearances, yet they are in reality, simple once we set our focus on doing them. As you increase involvement and practice, what seems, by all accounts, to be an overwhelming undertaking, ends up simpler as the dread decreases and in the long run vanishes. You may state that carrying out the responsibility is more difficult than one might expect. For this situation, before carrying out responsibility, consider something exceptionally wonderful and pleasant. It could be a most loved leisure activity or action, for example, an outing to your preferred excursion recognize, a fantastic view to your preferred b-ball, or different games game, or even a melodic show. Consider the delight and the fervor you felt on those events. Along these lines, at whatever point you consider the undertaking, supplant the negative feelings with the positive feelings of satisfaction, joy and fervor you felt as you recalled those glad events. Be that as it may, in the event that you don't have confidence in yourself, odds are you won't probably do it. In this way, ponder your capacity to achieve the undertaking and afterward envision yourself prevailing at doing it.

Take, for example, a few people who have never determined, have dread or anxiety about driving. In any case, when they start taking driving exercises and getting in the driver's seat, picking up understanding and practice with driving in safe regions, driving seems simpler as the dread vanishes. Regarding starting a characteristic eye exercise program, the feelings of trepidation are frequently unjustified in light of the fact that a program of activities to improve visual perception is very simple and fun. We should make a correlation with Yoga. While Yoga is extremely valuable as far as mitigating pressure and anxiety and improving our general wellbeing, it requires a wealth of vitality and adaptability to play out a portion of the stances; teaches that many individuals discover very testing to stay aware of.

A characteristic vision improvement program then again uses simple and basic eye practice methods that include eye developments that require negligible vitality to perform. You don't have to figure out how to keep up equalization or ace methods that require incredible adaptability to prevail at the program. For instance, here is an example of a straightforward eye practice strategy to improve partial blindness: Inhale and breathe out all through the whole course of this activity. Hold a pen around three crawls from your nose. Keep up your attention on a little purpose of this pen as you move the pen out to a manageable distance. Drop the pen to your lap, and afterward rehash a couple of times. This system improves the centering intensity of the eyes in an exceptionally straightforward and simple way.

Don't allow obstacles related to fear and anxiety to hold you back from achieving your vision improvement goals. Ultimately, by turning negatives into positives, you can replace fear and anxiety with the motivation that is needed to help you to achieve not only vision improvement goals but all of life's goals in general.

FEW SIMPLE TIPS YOU CAN DO

Dread and anxiety are among the feared things a great many people would prefer not to experience throughout everyday life. We as a whole have our feelings of dread, and that can be unique in from one individual to another. Truth be told there are the individuals who fear things that other individuals would not regularly fear.

It is entirely expected to feel dread however. Truth be told, it prepares ourselves in planning for what is to come and it encourages us to get ready to meet the vulnerabilities and address the difficulties of life. In any case, giving apprehension and anxiety a chance to control your life might be an alternate story. It can likewise demolish a decent quality life that you can't appreciate. On the off chance that you are experiencing apprehension and you are faced with the test of beating trepidation and anxiety, here are a couple of tips that you may discover helpful.

1. Practice unwinding methods to enable you to chop down the apprehensions and anxiety that you are feeling. One of the basic approaches to quiet yourself is to adapt profound breathing activities, learn contemplation just as other unwinding systems. Remember that albeit a little dread can support you, a lot of it or steady dread can push you to settle on terrible choices and can influence an amazing nature. Reflection is one of the unwinding procedures that can help a great deal in defeating apprehension and anxiety; however, ensure that you get familiar with the right method to contemplate and that you gain from the specialists too.

2. Stay away from medications, caffeine, and liquor. These are stimulants that can likewise intensify your sentiments of anxiety and dread. On the off chance that you are somebody attempting to quiet yourself or somebody attempting to unwind and dispose of dread, at that point, you need to consider that you have

these components in your eating routine. In the event that you do, you may need to eliminate them or get proficient assistance particularly if you have been smoking for quite a while or you have been dependent on medications or liquor for a long while as of now. Obviously, there are establishments that can assist you with it, yet it really begins with you.

3. Have an ordinary exercise. As anxiety and dread can draw out a blend of pressure hormones and other states of mind disturbing synthetic concoctions in the body and having normal exercise can enable your body to discharge more temperament improving synthetics and endorphins that can enable you to manage anxiety and dread. Obviously, exercise can likewise help a great deal in quieting your nerves and is additionally an awesome diversion that can get your psyche off your feelings of trepidation and discharge negative energies that encompass you.

4. Getting treatments in conquering apprehension and anxiety. If dread and anxiety have been a noteworthy block in your life, perhaps the best thing that you can do to take out these emotions is to go into an intellectual social treatment. This is typically done by a specialist and getting a progression of these treatments can genuinely be valuable in dispensing with these undesirable apprehensions and nerves throughout everyday life.

These are only a couple of the things that you can do to manage anxiety. Keep in mind the faster you can get arrangements, the quicker you can also appreciate a decent quality life.

WHY DO PEOPLE WITH LOW SELF-ESTEEM SUFFER FROM FEAR AND ANXIETY?

Individuals with low self-regard commonly experience psychological mistreatment as malignant prodding, mockery, unjustifiable decisions and analysis during their developing years.

Being continually made to feel shame, blame and disgracefulness for carrying on uniquely in contrast to what others need, they have generally expected comparative medications even as a grown-up. This places them in a condition of steady hyper-carefulness about how individuals would respond to them, which further worsens their sentiments of fear and anxiety of being mocked and shunned.

At that point, there is the anxiety of not realizing what they need to do to fit in with the group. However, this absence of knowing does not propel the individual with low self-regard to assemble the required data for them to connect easily with others. They don't see that they have the alternative of taking classes or perusing up certain materials to procure the vital aptitudes.

Or maybe, they see this absence of learning as something interesting to themself and an indication of a noteworthy blemish as a part of their character. They neglect to understand that those with solid self-regard are additionally uninformed in numerous subjects yet are not modest to concede their absence of learning and request help all the time.

Thus, the individual with low self-regard denies themselves from getting to the vital data out of fear of seeming unusual. To adapt to their sentiments of anxiety, they may lie or think of reasons for dodging awkward circumstances, which are regularly many.

For example, during a get-together assembling, John's previous secondary classmates were having an enthusiastic discourse about the monetary securities exchange. John felt humiliated on the grounds that he hadn't a due about what they were stating. Rather than conceding that the subject was new to him and utilized this chance to build his mindfulness, he immediately pardoned himself for fear of being 'discovered'.

The individual with low self-regard needs to get this:-

• Everyone has humiliating or embarrassing moments.

• Every individual has encountered incalculable dismissals throughout their life, in different zones, for example, during school selection tests, prospective employee meet-ups or connections.

• Everyone commits errors. No one is impeccable.

A solid self-regard is your claim. No one has a low self-regard from birth. It was found out on account of others.

The best thing you can do to defeat low self-regard is to for all time expel the impact of past molding. Cutting edge mental systems like Hypnotherapy and Emotional Freedom Technique can do a great deal to assist you with releasing the sentiments of disgrace, blame and dishonor appended to your negative beloved recollections. When these emotions are discharged, sound self-regard will be re-established, then fear and anxiety will turn into a relic of times gone by.

Chapter 7: Surround Yourself With

Positivity

Are your surroundings energizing? Are the people you have around you filled with positive energy and give you joy? Sometimes it doesn't matter how you are feeling these outside influences can just drag you down and leave you feeling insecure and empty.

Consider the people in your life, do some people just leave you exhausted after spending time with them? You know the type, energy suckers! Imagine a vampire that feeds on energy and leaves you flat and lifeless once they have fed. The thing is, these people are a direct reflection of your own personal beliefs about yourself.

They are drawn to you because they sense your insecurities and use them to feed their own negativity. So, what can you do to change the type of people that are drawn to you? The good news is that as you improve your self-belief you also improve your vibes. This will attract more positive people to you and improve the energy that surrounds you.

Simply put if you have negative feelings of self-doubt you will attract the energy vampires yet if you feel great about yourself you will attract positive energy.

Here are three life-changing tips to attract positive people to your "vibes"

Believe in yourself

Think of the people you know who are self-confident and positive. You are immediately aware that they have confidence that shines like a light in a dark room. Accept who you are and embrace your strengths, talents, and abilities. Have a daily talk with yourself and be kind. Tell yourself you look great and that outfit looks amazing on you. Be positive and you will attract positive relationships.

Forgive freely

Holding a grudge is a surefire way to display negative energy. Forgiving people is not a weakness, in fact, it is a strength. Letting go of resentment and emotional pain frees you from becoming stuck in the moment. Once you have forgiven yourself or others for mistakes you are free to explore a future free from negative memories. Recognize that you can learn from difficult life lessons and grow as a person and you will shift to higher energy plane. This, in turn, will attract like-minded people into your life.

Appreciate others

Sharing appreciation of others encourages them to grow closer to you and form stronger bonds. Celebrate the success of others and encourage them to reach greater heights instead of feeling resentful of their success. When you achieve your goals, you will have supportive set of friends just waiting to help you celebrate as well!

It is highly rewarding to be surrounded by positive people, but it takes practice. When you feel a negative thought entering your space you must replace it with a self-affirming thought. Make it a natural practice to think of yourself as a magnificent being and at home with other magnificent people!

Of course, your relationships are significant but there are other ways to create positivity around you. Here are some simple tricks to introduce a positive element to your surroundings.

Nature

A display of fresh flowers can lift even the dullest room. Bringing nature into the home or workplace can be refreshing and give you a positive focus. A potted plant or a bouquet of spring flowers will look great on your desk or in your living space. If you have allergies or other restrictions, you can use natural fabrics or materials to create a calming environment. A beautiful wooden bowl or a cashmere throw will allow you to appreciate nature's beauty.

Visual aids

Having a visual perception of your positivity surrounding you is essential. Display framed photos of your family and loved ones will help you tackle difficult times and motivate you. Maybe you are inspired by people in the media or even places you want to visit. Use your goals to motivate you by placing images in your eye line. They will help you put in the extra effort if you are feeling down and just need some motivation. Surround yourself with beauty and fond memories and you will always have a smile on your face!

Music and media

What you see around you is important but so is what you hear. If music is your passion, then make powerful playlists to suit different occasions. Choose inspiring, high energy tracks to listen to when you need a boost. Have a playlist to relax to, even one to eat too! If you love music use it to inspire you and carry you to the next place. The beauty is you can take it just about anywhere, the car, the gym, work, and home. If music isn't your thing you can listen to other types of audio, try an inspirational speech by someone you admire. Catch up on current affairs by tuning into news outlets and informational podcasts. The bottom line is don't neglect your ears!

Quality entertainment

How you spend your leisure time should also be considered. Pick up a good book and immerse yourself fully for a couple of hours. Self-help books are great but sometimes you just need to lose yourself in a great story. Become the hero and learn how to adapt their qualities to help your own personal journey. Alternatively watch some quality TV or a movie. There is a wealth of excellent shows and movies that can help you enjoy your downtime and also be inspired.

Spread positivity

Be free with compliments and give genuine feedback to others. If someone does something that you find impressive then share your sentiments. Even holding the door open for someone can make their day. Giving up your seat and offering to allow someone to go in front of you in a queue may seem insignificant but they are both positive twists on life. Volunteering is a great way to give back to the community and spread positivity. Helping people less fortunate than yourself will also help you appreciate what you have and the love that surrounds you.

Quotes

Positive affirmations help you reach higher levels of positivity and should be used daily (we will cover this later!) but quotes can also inspire you. Create your own personal life motto and display it prominently, use inspirational words from your favorite people. Avoid negative energy by surrounding yourself with positivity. These quotes can also be amusing, life doesn't have to be too serious, take a look at these funny life quotes:

"You know you're old when the candles cost more than the cake" Bob Hope

"The fact we're all different is the one thing we have in common" Justin Young

"Stop worrying about the world ending today, it's already tomorrow in Australia" Charles M Schultz

If you are looking for inspiration the world is an open book! Search for words to inspire you and fill you with hope and use them daily.

Chapter 8: Trouble With Over Thinking

Have you ever been in the shower or blow drying your hair or driving while you were thinking about what someone said or did… or perhaps even something you said or did? And in the thinking about it you created a bigger story about it than it was? No? Am I alone in that? I suspect not. The places may be different, but many of us caught up from time to time in over-thinking and over-analyzing.

I recently caught myself doing this exact thing. I created my own personal mind-drama…. And the more I thought about it and talked about it, the bigger it got. And because I like to understand anything that triggers me, I kept analyzing myself and trying to figure out why I was feeling the way I was feeling and I also began to analyze and assume how the other party may be thinking and feeling.

I created a whole mind drama. And the reason I say " mind drama" is because fortunately it was all just in my mind, and I did not exacerbate it by talking about it to anyone who would listen. However, as I'm sure you all know, this can happen as well. In trying to feel "right" with how we are feeling, we often share the story with others in hopes they will validate our feelings.

Regardless, even though it was not outward drama, it was drama all the same for me. I was over-thinking what I had said, and how I was feeling. And once having spoken to the individual this situation involved, I could not help but laugh at my silliness when I learned that she had not been thinking any of the things I had created in my story.

The reason I am sharing this is because we need to become aware that the assumptions and analyzing that we make about what others are thinking or how they may be feeling are skewed and filtered through our own emotions. Because of this we jump to conclusions that may not be true and can be very harmful both to ourselves and any others involved.

For this reason, I am a huge advocate of speaking up and expressing your feelings in order to get clarification. But most of all I think we need to catch ourselves when our thoughts begin to override our mind. It happens to the best of us, no one is immune and self awareness is the key.

SUFFERING FROM OVER THINKING ADDICTION

Do you ever over thing things? Do you get caught up in mental cycles of negativity or fear that keep you from living fully? Does your mind race like a hamster wheel and you just wish you could step off?

Did it ever occur to you that you might be addicted thinking? If so you are not alone. It is estimated that the average person has between 50,000 to 60,000 thoughts per day.

Yet, how many of those thoughts are helpful? How many do you really need? How many are even true?

Though most people are unaware of it, addiction to thinking is the number one addiction affecting us humans today. And, it just may be the driving force behunde all of our other addictions.

Symptoms of over thinking

Here are the symptoms you may not have associated with over-thinking:

Constant worrying about what you did in the past or what might happen in the future

A incessant voice in your head that comment on everything

Keeping the radio or TV on as a constant background

Needing to keep your mind busy

Constantly checking your face book, Twitter, texts and email

Discomfort with silence, stillness, and inactivity

Discomfort with feelings and body sensations

Trouble sleeping meditating or relaxing deeply

Feeling there always too much to do & ever enough time

Feeling a constant subtle stress that never lets up

So, what is behind addiction to thinking? why is it there?

What drive, it? If we knew what that was, maybe we could put a stop to it and the stress it causes!

There is a two pronged false belief that traps us in our thoughts:

We believe that our thoughts represent reality and,

We believe that we are our thoughts

Without us being, aware of it these two false beliefs makes us slaves to the mental fabrications we call thoughts

Mental fabrications?

Yes, that is right. Our problems begin when we mistakenly believe that our thoughts represent reality.

If that were the case, of course, thinking would be as important as it seems. It would be how we know what is real and possible in our lives.

Yet, thinking does not, in fact, represent reality. Instead thinking interprets, categorizes, and organizes reality. Thinking is not about representing Reality at all, it is about analyzing reality and organizing it for action.

Chapter 9: Cultivate Healthy Habits

Rethink Resolutions

The issue with resolutions is that they have a yearly expiration date. It's nonsensical to put a one-year limit on a practice that will deliver us a lifetime of health.

Several more research studies demonstrate that the way to excellent wellbeing is a term that specialists call "lifestyle medication" — rolling out improvements in diet, exercise, and stress management.

It doesn't matter if you are working in Corporate America or slaving ceaselessly as a full-time mother, it is very simple to fall into an undesirable way of life these days. Do you frequently end up feeling exhausted or disheartened? Have you always had the need to completely change yourself to improve things? However, are you uncertain about where to begin?

Fortunately, like your daily espresso or how you binge reruns of Orange Is the New Black, developing sound habits is as simple as arranging a meeting with a co-worker while shopping in the produce area of your local supermarket. In some cases, we all need a little push of inspiration.

How would we develop solid habits and roll out positive improvements in our lives? We have two choices: we can relinquish something that isn't working, or we can present something new that will.

For instance, we can stop (or seriously limit) our consumption of French fries, or we can focus on consistently eating an additional daily serving of veggies. This type of decision brings about a progressively nourishing diet.

It might be useful to quit unhealthy practices to remain balanced; we should replace them with healthier options, such as substituting a plate of mixed greens for French fries when eating out.

To be effective, we should make space for change by saving time and energy to take part in new practices. A lot of us are totally over-booked, living on autopilot and moving excitedly through the days and hours, taking part in similar exercises and thoughts and doing similar things again and again, even though they are not working.

One meaning of craziness is to continue doing what you are doing again and again while anticipating an alternate outcome. What number of us are doing only that, possibly without acknowledging it — eating the same unhealthy foods while wanting to get in shape or hoping to feel invigorated while never setting aside some time and effort to work out?

To transform our mentality, we initially need to see what isn't working or what we need to get rid of. At that point, we should intentionally focus on deduction and carrying on in an unexpected way. Focusing on every little detail and rolling out little improvements can help move us toward our most profound wants and needs. We don't have to overpower ourselves with a lot of modifications at the same time. Little changes can prompt huge outcomes after some time.

Every day is another chance to start once more, but we can gather momentum just by getting started. I urge you to start where you are. What do you need more of? What do you need less of? In what capacity will you start to develop it?

Harness that inspiration and start making dependable, amazing changes that will improve your psychological and physical wellbeing.

Approach these changes with strong, positive, continual intent, and dump the New Year's resolutions. This time stamped, brief pledges will simply help you, in the best-case scenario, to develop temporary positive results. Alternatively, use the power of the New Year to create strong intentions that you can reiterate once per day and maintain for a lifetime. The customized, repetitive, and solid nature of inclinations is the best approach to flourishing in the long-term. Everything considered, what we do daily matters more than what we do from time to time. Here are some keys to developing a more beneficial way of life for 2019 and beyond.

Start Again (Without Any Preparation)

We've dismissed the basic elements of strong living and put our trust in "cutting edge" and complex programs, ricocheting from one program to another. In any case, by what method may we work on the fundamentals if we haven't generally enabled them to accomplish something stunning? This year, maintain a strategic distance from these examples and stick with the tried and true.

Certified food is stimulating, sustaining, prevents disease, and boosts attitudes—all that we need to live a long, strong, and cheerful life. Fiber-rich whole grains, extraordinary proteins, and strong fats, for instance, nuts, seeds, olives, and avocado—all of these rich, whole foods are perfectly packaged with the supplements, minerals, fiber, cell fortifications, and other essential elements that we need to prosper. In any case, mulls over exhibiting a normal portion of our eating routine is included ultra-dealt with sustenance's that are without important enhancements just as contain unsafe and phony included substances.

Water: The human body is around 65-70% water, an undeniable indicator of its importance to human health. Water supports the essential activity of every organ in the body, from transporting food, regulating the body's temperature, repairing the tissue, detoxifying the body, etc. Sufficient water replenishment is essential to perfect health, yet research indicates that a striking 75% of Americans are working under a wearisome absence of hydration.

Rest: Sleep is simply our body's opportunity to fix, patch up, and restore, yet we are more occupied with our mobile phones than we are about our most critical device of all: our body! As to flourishing, rest is routinely under-recognized. Studies show that over 33% of the U.S masses are anxious. Rest is as equally important as sustenance for improving health. Believe it or not, rest influences what we want, what we eat, our supplement use, our worry hormones, our weight, our imperativeness level, our perspective, and our education level.

Improvement. Our bodies were created to move, to act, and to achieve our goals, yet consistently, we are becoming progressively stationary. Studies measure that American adults spend, on average, 13 hours sitting each day, and only20% meet the CDC's physical development rules. While it's true that you can't work off a habit of unhealthy eating, there are a many important reasons to move your body. Standard exercise advances rest quality, improves academic performance, improves processing, keeps weight down, redesigns physical presentations, and supports progressively valuable sustenance choices.

Breathe. Our masses are living under perpetual pressure, anyway really, the more that we take care of ourselves, the more we can ask of ourselves. "Unplugging" improves proficiency, imagination, health, and fulfillment. Whether it's yoga, reflection, reading a book, cleaning, drinking a cup of tea, or doing an enema, taking a break to loosen up and reset is essential to our health and satisfaction.

Recognize What Areas That We Need to Work on for Long-Term Wellbeing.

Most of us realize that we have to eat healthily, workout, get lots of rest, and drink heaps of water to lead a healthy lifestyle. Several individuals believe they are making a better than average effort to be healthy. Notwithstanding, a large portion of us are not. One examination found that only three percent of adults meet every one of the criteria to maintain a healthy lifestyle. According to scientists, there are four keys to healthy living, including:

Not smoking.

Maintaining a healthy weight (a BMI of 18-25) or effectively getting in shape to achieve this.

Eating a minimum of five servings of vegetables and fruits daily.

Exercising for a minimum of 30 minutes, five times each week.

Few of us really accomplish every one of these things. And although these are significant, there is a lot more to being healthy than meeting the criteria stated above. It's likewise about having a positive frame of mind, a positive mental self-image, achieving psychological wellness, and spending time with your loved ones. In this way, before you decide to work on self-improvement, select which areas you want to fortify. Start with what you need to work on most and work your way up.

Recognize What Works For You.

Your ability to lead a healthy way of life will rely upon formulating ideas/strategies that work with your character. Pause for a moment to think about the times that you have succeeded and the times that you have battled with things. What conditions were most useful to you and encouraged you to make your best effort?

What circumstances did you find diverting? What prevented you from working toward and achieving your objectives? Whatever your objectives are, before you can make changes to your way of life, you must realize where you're coming from and have an understanding of the reasons that you would like to make changes. Recognize what works for you and what doesn't.

Break Unhealthy Habits.

The things we do all the time, from brushing our teeth to eating certain snacks, regularly form our habits. The initial move toward changing any conduct is to assess our present habits.

If you're prone to practicing each morning, that is great. If you're prone to purchasing a pack of chips and a soft drink each evening that is definitely not. You must search for approaches to break that pattern and build up new patterns while proceeding with your healthy habits. Start rolling out little day-by-day improvements. Pack healthy foods to take to work. Carry a refillable water bottle with you so that you can remain hydrated for the duration of the day.

Modify Your Approach

While the five crucial segments to healthy living are deceivingly simple, they are often difficult to achieve. What we need is a detailed plan to truly implement these basics vigorously in our daily lives. Furthermore, we don't require just any plan; we need one that takes into account our individual qualities and tendencies. There is no one-size-fits-all formula for healthy living. Healthy living is achieved by finding the practices that work best for you. Here's how you can achieve a healthy lifestyle that works for you:

Become More Self-Aware

While the basics of healthy living are the same for all humankind, how we complete them will vary from person to person. Your ability to thrive will depend upon how well that you can find techniques that line up with your personality type and your individual characteristics. It's much less complex to change your methods to fit with your character than it is to endeavor to wedge yourself into an inflexible structure that goes again sty our nature.

Do you need duty, or do you challenge responsibilities?

Do you lean toward disengagement or social settings?

Do you lean toward consistency or variety?

Are you a night person or a morning person?

Which strategy do you prefer: coordinating or maintaining a strategic distance from someone/something?

Are you organized, or do you like to live carelessly?

Would you like to make enormous steps or small advances?

How you answer these questions will empower you to recognize the best frameworks for bringing back the essentials. For example, if you are someone that requires obligation, seeking regular exercise classes or finding an activity buddy may empower you to maintain a regular exercise plan. If you're someone that prefers variability, having a structured, detailed exercise plan may be troubling and stressful for you; perhaps a Class-Pass enlistment offering a variety of classes and a flexible schedule will keep you engaged.

Use Habit Hacks

Since you have now decided what habits you would like to form, you are ready to start forming them. Molding new habits can be as difficult as breaking old ones, but there are various methods and strategies that you can use to combat this. Here are a few helpful tips to help start you in the right direction:

Focus on every element of the habits that you would like to achieve and separate them into smaller, more manageable parts. This will shield you from feeling overwhelmed and compromised from trying to change too much, too soon, and it will reframe the inclination into a task so basic that it is simple to achieve. For example, if you drink ten glasses of water in a day, remind yourself to drink a huge glass of water every hour.

When a task is scheduled, it becomes necessary, encouraging us to manage our time around it. We can also obtain a sense of achievement from crossing tasks off our list when we are finished. Create an hourly event in your calendar to remind you to take a brief walk and grab a glass of water, and include your step-by-step activities in your schedule.

Redoing: Recreate your space to create the best environmental conditions for your success. Remove things from your space that trigger you to revert to unhealthy habits and replace them with things that aid you in developing healthy habits. For example, give your kitchen a makeover; place healthy food choices at eye level, and store less healthy food son the top row of your cabinet, out of arm's range. Assemble your duffel pack the night before an activity.

Make Room in Your Schedule for Both Work and Play

Numerous business visionaries guarantee that work–life balance is a legend. The act of creating balance in our lives frequently constrains us to make concessions. It feels like a giant balancing act, and we're overwhelmed with commitments and stress. To an ever-increasing extent, organizations understand that we have to address life matters while at work and that we need flexibility in our work routines.

The fact is, rather than concentrating on the limits where your work life ends and your individual life starts, search for approaches to mix a fulfilling and combination of both. Concentrate on making reliable, sound, positive decisions that mirror your qualities, duties and objectives over the course of your life.

Oversee pressure.

Our reality is that we live in profoundly dynamic and pressurized conditions. Our lives pass by so quickly that it's frequently a battle to keep up.

This puts a lot of pressure on us. It's essential that we recognize which things are within our locus of control and which things aren't. For instance, getting a punctured tire is not within your control, but getting a terrible audit for imperfect work is within your control.

You can decrease and manage your worry by assuming responsibility for the things that you can control. Then, when unforeseen upsetting occasions occur, you will be relaxed and focused enough to concentrate on and take care of those issues without becoming overpowered. You can likewise participate in relaxation techniques, for example, meditation and breathing deeply, to enable you to oversee feelings of stress.

Slow Down and Stay in the Moment.

Many of us are so focused on our occupations and regular undertakings that we neglect to appreciate the present moment.

Take a moment to slow down and appreciate your surroundings, such as the sound of giggling, how the sun feels all over, and how your legs feel as you walk.

Make time for gratitude at several points in your day.

The business world is orderly and requires steady advancement and examination; you are only as good as your latest achievement. Figure out how to appreciate each step of this process. Doing so will add to your sense of achievement and will make the ultimate result considerably more satisfying.

A way of life ought to be something that supports your life objectives. Take a step back and ask yourself: What would you like to accomplish, get involved in, or create in your lifetime? How can you pursue your interests and desires and accomplish your life aspirations? Regardless of whether it's raising a family, venturing to the far corners of the planet, or beginning your very own organization, each aspiration turns out to be increasingly achievable when you accomplish wellbeing and prosperity.

Chapter 10: Mindfulness And Positive

Thinking

If you have dipped in the sector of positive psychology, you must have discovered the most popular topics of today, which is mindfulness. It is a broad part of human psychology, which has evolved in the last few years.

What is mindfulness?

It is nothing but the act of maintaining all the moments of your very own feelings, thoughts, surrounding environment along with bodily sensations via the lens of nurturing and gentle nature. Each and every human being in this world is wired towards the aspects of negativity. You can easily get caught up in the cycle of rumination, along with worrying and imagining about each and every possible outcome of your future. This often leads to an increased amount of anxiety along with lots of stress.

But, when you keep all your thoughts moving in the direction of positiveness, it will not only make you feel good at that very moment, but it can also help in reducing your degree of sadness to a great extent. Moreover, it can also provide you with the one and only thing that all human beings require for keeping up with their lives: HOPE. The more you engage yourself in employing positive thinking and mindfulness in your life, the longer the efforts will be lasting.

Meditation based on mindfulness

You must have come across the term 'mindfulness meditation.' If you think that what is the real difference between mindfulness and meditation based on mindfulness, then there really isn't any such major difference. Mindfulness is referred in the general attempts for incorporating more amount of mindfulness in the life of an individual whereas, meditation based on mindfulness is the kind of practice which is often seen as the most stereotypical form of meditation with you sitting with your legs crossed and eyes closed while engaging in the activity of basic meditation for a certain time period.

Typically, mindfulness meditation and mindfulness often refer to the same kind of concept in which you stay aware and open up your inner-self and also allow all your thoughts along with your feelings to take place without any kind of judgment. The only form of distinction which can be found in between the two is that the concept of mindfulness meditation comes with the connotation of turning out to be a kind of practice which is time-constrained in nature.

The most common question which is often found regarding mindfulness is that whether it is a trait or a state? This question is of utter importance for someone who actually dabbles in mindfulness. Whether if it is a strength or a trait, permanent or less changeable is often a debate.

Need for mindfulness and positive thinking Have you wondered ever about what it actually means to live at the present moment? It is true that all of us are available right now at the current moment. But, only 10% of us are actually right here. All of us are actually living within our minds and thoughts. Human beings exist in a state of day to daydream where you are not connected with the world in actual and nor with your own being. Instead of that, all of us are actually preoccupied with all our past memories, where we are busy churning our worries and thoughts about the future along with the reactions and the judgments of a few of the things which we actually see. You are missing out a majority of your life, which ultimately leaves you in feeling empty, shallow, and also unsettled in life. That is when you need to learn to be mindful and also to be at present. Let's have a look at some of the ways with which you can easily practice mindfulness in your regular life.

Eating mindfully: When you actually gulp down your meal while being distracted by the computer, TV, or any form of constant conversation, you are actually missing out on the delicious taste and attractive smell of the food. You are also very less likely to actually feel nourished and satisfied after having a sumptuous meal as you literally missed out on the very fact of what you actually ate. In simple words, do not try to do 100 things at a time when you actually sit for having your meal. Try to focus on what you are eating as it has been proven that when you eat well, you feel good. Having a tasty meal can make you feel positive and happy when you actually have a meal in an enjoyable way.

Walking down the road mindfully: There is a saying, 'walk in a way as if you are embracing the earth right with your feet.' In simple words, when you are out on the road all alone, try to pay attention to all the significant movements of your body along with the surroundings. Notice the moment as your feet connects with the ground and then leave it again. All that you need to do is to just observe what is actually going around you. When you try to take a walk all by yourself, you can actually connect with yourself in a better way than you can do at any other point of time.

Try to feel everything around you, the sounds, the sights, and the lives which are unfolding around you. If you are having negative thoughts or you are just ruminating, try going out for a short walk where you can connect your inner-self. You will be actually amazed to find out the results as you will be able to connect your heart with your mind like never before. You are needed to understand that you are your own best friend. So, try to connect with your inner friend for getting the most out of your life and enjoy the same to the fullest.

Observing the way in which you breathe: One single breath in and out can actually work like meditation. The way in which you breathe occurs rhythmically and naturally. When you actually start to pay attention to the way in which you breathe, it can take you right out of your mind and will let you into your very own body. You will feel free momentarily from all the churning kinds of thoughts, fears, and worries in your mind, and you will also be able to recognize your true self by getting in touch with your inner soul and not with your regular kind of thoughts.

Connecting with all your senses: The human senses- smell, taste, touch, sight, and sound- are actually the gateway of getting into the current moment. But, at times, when you remain lost in your thoughts, you will most likely not experience the things which your senses are sensing or picking up for your mind. You can achieve this by doing the simplest things, such as pausing for soaking up the fantastic aroma of your coffee, the salty kind of ocean wind, the diversity in your neighborhood, the beauty of flowers, and many others.

You can also achieve mindfulness by noticing how the clothing is feeling against your torso or body, the clean and soft bed sheets on the skin every morning, the comfort that you get as you kiss your lover, and various other things. All that you need to do is to just put a little amount of love along with attention to the simplest tasks of your everyday life, and you will actually be amazed when you will realize the amount of peace and joy that you can actually bring up for yourself.

Taking a pause in between the actions: You can try to pause at some of the simplest events in your life and just listen to the inner meaning. You can pause and feel your body weight in the chair right before you start working on your desk. The primary goal is to give mini pauses to your life in between various actions throughout your day, which can actually help you in reaching out to your inner-self, clear up your mind, and can also provide you with a fresh form of energy for all the new forms of tasks.

Listening wholeheartedly: Most of us do not even listen to the people who are actually speaking to us just because we are engaged in the thought of what should be said next, judging all the things which are being said by various people or just getting lost in our world of daydreams. The very next time, when you find yourself in a meaningful conversation, try to make it your primary goal to actually listen to what is being said by the other person in conversation instead of just getting lost on your very own thoughts. This will also help in getting the actual message of the conversation as mindfulness is all about living in the present.

Getting lost in the flow of doing all the things which you love: Each and every one of us has certain kinds of activities in our life which we love doing the most. Such activities actually help in connecting with our inner spirit and also help in bringing us alive. For you, it can be dancing, cooking, gardening, singing, painting, writing, swimming, cycling, etc. People often tend to love all those things which they often find losing themselves in. You can incorporate more flow in your activities in your daily routine, and you will find that your happiness will be reaching new heights.

Meditating daily: Nothing can be better than meditation. When you start meditating regularly, you will come across various benefits like an increase in the levels of happiness, energy, inner peace, and inspiration. When you will find yourself getting lost in the thoughts or when you start overthinking, just take out some time and meditate. It is not needed to be more than just 10 minutes and only this amount of time in meditation can bring you wonders. It can provide your life with a positive impact. It will help you in strengthening up your muscles of mindfulness so that it becomes easier for you to be in the present moment all throughout your day.

Traveling or mixing up your entire routine: There are various reasons why people feel so amazing when they are on holidays. When you visit a new place, you will become more mindful naturally and be in the present moment as there are various new sounds, sights, and smells in which you can soak up your inner-self. When you travel, your senses will take over your mind for a moment, and it will result in freeing up your mind right after that. Do not have any travel plans currently? No worries as you can mix up your entire routine for having the same kind of effect.

Try to take a different road, stop by a new café, try to visit a newly opened place or try to opt for something which you haven't done before ever in your life like cooking on your own without anyone's help, scuba diving, and various other activities. When you opt for new activities at regular intervals, you will find yourself to be more confident and creative than before, and your mind will open up to new opportunities and will be soaking in all that it can get.

Observing all your emotions and thoughts: You are not actually your thoughts but the observer of all the thoughts. The very fact that you listen to all of them depicts that they are not actually you. You are someone separate and much higher than your thoughts. When you be aware of your thoughts and observe without judgmental eyes, you can be a part of the present. As you observe all your thoughts, you are required to resists all your temptations from getting carried away with them right down a narrow into your future or past. So, do not just get carried away with your thoughts.

Benefits of practicing mindfulness

Mindfulness comes along with several benefits. The studies have found out that mindfulness can actually alter the human physiology of our minds and bodies in various ways so that they can be healed, strengthened, and protected. Let's have a look at some of the benefits of practicing mindfulness.

Lowers down stress: Mindfulness helps in lowering down your physiological markers of deep stress and also helps in improving the ability of your brain to manage stress. It is done by improving the connectivity in those areas of your brain which is essential for executing all the controls.

Helps in restoring emotional balance: Emotional incidents have the ability to knock you down from your balance. The damage which is done comes in great intensity, which can devastate your mental makeup. Mindfulness helps in improving your rate of recovery from any kind of emotional situation simply by keeping a check of the emotional part of the brain.

Helps in reducing anxiety: It has been found from various studies can mindfulness can reduce the degree of anxiety in adults by up to a rate of 40%. It is done by increasing the amount of activity in that part of the brain, which processes all the emotional and cognitive forms of information along with that part of the brain, which controls the situations of worrying.

Helps in reducing physical pain: It has been proved that mindfulness can easily reduce the physical form of pain without even activating the opioid system of the body. It also helps in reducing the potential for any kind of side effects of addictive nature. This is really beneficial for you if you experience physical pain very often and is particularly helpful for those who have actually built up a good system of tolerance for opiate-based drugs.

Helps in reducing depression: It readily helps in dealing with depression as it helps in opening up your mind so that you can soak in all the positive energy from your surroundings and feel more motivated.

Helps in improving quality of sleep: You can easily improve your sleep quality by practicing mindfulness regularly. It also helps in reducing fatigue along with insomnia.

Helps in improving concentration: It helps in improving your executive form of attention and thus helps in improving your ability to concentrate on your task. Mindfulness also helps in ignoring all forms of distractions, which are most likely to act as the barriers in your way to success. Mindfulness comes with the same effects as undergoing therapy from a therapist. It helps in the building up of a positive form of energy, which ultimately helps in improving your senses.

Chapter 11: Myths About Worry

1. Worrying helps people solve problems: This is a belief that worrying will make people more prepared to face specific problems, and it also helps us react better to certain issues when they arise. This myth has been making the rounds for an extended period. Some people believe that when you worry about someone or a particular thing, you tend to be able to solve problems comfortably and faster. It is also believed that when you worry to a certain extent, you will be able to react to things better. There are a lot of people that find it hard to face their problems head on, and this myth says that it happens because they do not worry enough. For example, if you worry about a particular danger no matter what it is, this myth is telling you that you will be able to foresee and possibly avoid it when and if it finally comes.

2. Worrying protects people from experiencing bad emotions:

This is another myth that a lot of people use. They believe that worrying about something ahead of time will make it easier for them to bare when something finally happens (that's if it does). This is an absurd notion, but a lot of people believe that it works. They think that worrying beforehand protects them from guilt, disappointment, or deception. For example, if a woman has a husband and she constantly worries about her husband cheating on her, when it finally happens (that's if it does), it is not going to be that hard to bear because she already suspected it and thus the pain is not as bad as it ought to be. This myth is far from the truth. If you think that your husband is cheating on you and you eventually start getting worried, if it finally happens, the hurt is still going to be overwhelming. The fact that you had certain speculations about your partner's infidelity does not make the matter easier on you when you confirm your suspicions. This is why they say there are some questions that you do not want to know the answers to.

3. Worrying helps people motivate themselves:

Myths like these are some of the strangest ones out there. It says that when you worry about something around you, to a particular extent, it helps you become a better person because it motivates. Sounds a little strange right? For example, if you have a long list of chores or maybe just a to-do list, this myth says that if you worry about them enough, it will motivate you to want to get them done as soon as you possibly can. At this point, you will think that you have heard it all, but it is important to know that there are people out there that believe things like this. Worrying about something a lot is not going to motivate you to get it done faster or more effectively. You could worry about getting certain chores in the house done, and after three months, those chores are still the exact way they were when you started to worry about them. If you are going to get something done, you would. Worrying is not going to add to it.

4. Worrying can affect events:

These events can either be positive or negative events. The myths tell us that if we worry enough, certain activities that we worry about will not occur at all. This is one of the most absurd ones among all the myths. For example, if you worry that your children are going to get in an accident on their bikes when they are going to school every day, they won't. Which means that your worry is helping them stay out of danger so you should not stop worrying. This is one of the myths that encourages worrying a lot. Wait, are these people playing God or something? If these things worked, why are children in Cuba and the Philippines getting kidnapped when their parents get worried that they may get captured? These people believe these myths to the extent that it not only clouds their judgment but their reasoning as well. You cannot see a shovel and call it a spade. Look at what is right in front of you and say exactly what you see.

There are some instances of people sitting in their homes, worrying that a particular team they are rooting for will lose. They believe that when they all sit and worry together, that specific group will later come back victorious, meaning that their worries will change the outcome of the game. If this were real, then a lot of soccer fans would start worrying about their teams losing about three weeks before the main game.

5. Worrying shows that you care:

This myth is one of the most apparent myths out there because a lot of people use it, especially parents and family members, but it is far from the truth. Worrying is most times confused with care. When you worry a lot, it does not mean that you care a lot. For instance, if you keep on worrying that your child is not home by 6 p.m., it doesn't mean that you are caring about that person. You can worry less and still care about a person or a group of people. There are some people out there that believe that if you do not worry enough, you do not care enough. If you are one of those people, you need to get your ideas checked out like pronto. There are a lot of people out there that do not make a fuss about where their loved ones are. Those people care, but the thing is that they do not show it in ways that would seem absurd. When you make worrying look like caring, you will push a lot of people from you because they will think that you are not giving them enough space and that you are probably stalking their lives. So, loosen up a bit. You can care but make it reasonable.

6. Worrying is natural:

This is another myth that a lot of people use. Worrying is indeed natural, in the sense that it is universal. It is essential to know that the fact that it is natural does not mean that it is useful. There are a lot of things that are natural but are far from beneficial. Tooth decay, jealousy, and accidents are all natural, but that does not mean that they benefit anybody in any way. People that say this often do so because they want to justify their worry. It is not natural for people to worry because worry fragments the mind, breaks focus, and destroys inner peace. It's imperative to know that just because we tend to worry sometimes does not mean that we should feed that worry and make it bigger and bolder. For instance, if you worry about your kids or any member of your family and someone tells you that you are going overboard with the worry, do not tell the person that you worry only because it is natural and you have to.

7. Failure to worry can be dangerous:

A lot of parents use this. They say that when you fail to worry, it could be risky and hazardous. Even when we were kids, we were always taught to worry one way or the other without us even knowing about it. When our parents tell us to "look out" or "duck," we think that they say it because they can. They say it because they worry, and they unconsciously pass those traits to you. This is why you say the same things to your younger siblings, your friends, and even your kids. Failure to worry is far from risky. When you worry, you will not be able to make a rational decision and understand certain things. It is only going to be unsafe and dangerous when you do not have a still mind. If your mind is in the right place, you will be able to make decisions that will not be considered risky. It is imperative to know that a still mind is a mind that is capable of steady awareness, but a worried mind is just a mind that cannot assimilate anything.

8. When things go well, you'd better worry:

This myth is just out of this world. Why would you want to worry when everything is going well? Just know that you should be careful what you wish for because you might get it. You should not worry when things go well for you even if a lot of bad things have been coming your way for a while. You should be happy and excited to see good things coming in your direction, not worrying unnecessarily about them. When certain things go your way, it shows that you may be doing something right. Do not let your worries overcloud the extraordinary things that reveal themselves to you. This myth says that if you get a promotion in your office after wanting that promotion for a very long time, worry that the promotion is too good to be true. So, instead of you celebrating your promotion, you end up worrying if you can play the part and sometimes you worry about the fact that they could come up one day and demote you or in worst cases, even fire you.

Some of these myths are part of the reason why people think that worrying is good, and it could help you in so many ways but by now you know that's not true at all. If you are one of those people who believe in these kinds of myths, you must stop as soon as you can before you end up passing your notions and ideas to your friends and maybe your kids. That's if you haven't already done that.

Chapter 12: Affirmations

7.1   What Is Affirmations and How It Works

Affirmations have helped many people make significant changes in their lives and the people around them. Do they work for everyone? Why do some people have achieved success using this technique but some people do not get anything from it?

What are Affirmations?

Affirmations are positive and direct statements that help an individual overcome self-sabotaging and negative thoughts. It helps a person visualize and believe in their goals, dreams, and abilities. In other words, you are affirming to yourself and helping yourself make positive changes to your life goals.

Affirmations have the power to work because it can program a person's mind into believing a concept. The mind known not to know the difference between what is real or fantasy. That is why when you watch a movie; you tend to empathize with the characters on the screen even though you know it's just a movie. But as soon as you leave the cinema, you are back into reality but can't help feel sorry or happy for the characters.

There are both positive and negative affirmations and some of these affirmations such as being told you are smart when you were a child or being told that you are clumsy can stick with us in both our conscious or unconscious mind.

If a negative belief is firmly rooted in our subconscious mind, then it will have the ability to override any positive affirmation even when we aren't aware of it. This is one of the reasons why people do not believe in positive affirmations because it doesn't seem to be working. Their negative patterns are so high it just knocks out the sun! So how do we add affirmations into our daily life and how can we make them prevail above our negative thinking?

7.2 The Best Way to Practice Affirmations

Step 1- On a day that you are alone and not busy or distracted (if you don't have a time like this, then make one) list down all your negative qualities. Include any criticism that others have made of you and those that you have been holding onto. Remember that we all have flaws so do not judge. By acknowledging your mistakes, you can then move forward and work on your flaws, and you can make a shift in your life. When you write these down, take note to see if you are holding any grudges along the way or holding on to it. For example, do you feel tightness or dread in your heart?

Step 2- Begin to write out an affirmation on the positive aspect of your self-assessment. Use powerful statement words to beef up this assessment. Instead of saying 'I am worthy' say 'I am extremely cherished and remarkable.'

Step 3- Practice every day reading this affirmation loudly for five minutes at least three times a day in the morning, afternoon and at night before going to sleep. You can do this while shaving or putting your make up on, or when you are fixing yourself a cup of tea or if you are in the shower. At best, look in the mirror, so you look at yourself and repeat these positive statements. You can also write these affirmations in your notebook at any time you feel like it. Take note of how your writing changes over time. If we do not like something, often writing this down will encompass using smaller handwriting but if we right in big and bold letterings, we are increasing the affirmation of this. This is really a mindfulness journey to get to the agenda of positive affirmation.

Step 4- To enhance the impact, do body movements such as placing your hand on your heart when you felt uncomfortable writing out negative criticism of yourself in Step 1. As you work on reprogramming your mind to alter it from the concept of affirmation to a real and definite personification of the quality that you see.

Step 5- Get a friend or a coach to repeat these affirmations to you. For example, if they are saying that you are cherished and remarkable, and then connect this statement with your situations such as 'excellent colleague' or 'good fathering.' If you are not comfortable with doing this with someone, then look at your reflection in the mirror and reinforce your positive message.

Affirmations can be an incredibly powerful tool that can help you change your state of mind, alleviate your mood and more importantly, ingrain the changes your desire into your life. But for all of this to happen, you first need to identify the negative and work on getting rid of them in your life.

7.3 Types of Affirmations

Examples of Positive Affirmation

Here are some examples of positive affirmations that you can use to relate to the various areas of your development:

I know, accept and am true to myself

I believe in myself and have confidence in my decisions

I eat a balanced diet, exercise regularly and get plenty of rest

I always learn from my mistakes

I know I am capable of anything and can accomplish anything I set my mind to

I have flaws and I am not perfect but that's ok because I am human

I never, ever give up

I can adapt and accept what I have no control over

I make the best of every situation

I always look at the bright side of life

I enjoy life to the fullest

I stand up for what I believe in, my morals and my values

I treat others with respect and recognize their individuality

I can make a difference

I can practice understanding, patience, and compassion

I am always up to learn new things and be open-minded

I live in the moment and learn from my past and prepare for my future

These are just some of the positive affirmations that you can use to be optimistic and pursue a fulfilling and happy mindset. Have fun in creating your own affirmations or tailor the above to suit your needs and situation. Most of the affirmations above can be used daily to uplift, inspire and motivate you and those around you.

Apart from the ones above, here are five other types of affirmations that you can use that are more geared towards the situations that you are in:

Affirmations to believe in Career Success

We all want success in our careers and it is common to worry if you are not prepared or if you do not have the right skills. If you ever need affirmations before a job or promotion interview, here are some of them:

I'm perfect for this job. I have the right skills

I am confident, I have the experience and I have great persuasion skills

I have the ability to make a difference in this company

Affirmations to make you feel attractive

It is normal to sometimes feel like we are not handsome or beautiful. This is just low confidence. If you ever feel like you have low self-esteem, here are some affirmations to repeat to yourself:

I am beautiful both in and out

I am perfect just the way I am and I am proud of the way I look

I love the clothes I am in. I feel great today!

Affirmations to combat fear

Fear is something we all face and it can materialize for so many reasons. It can be a new job, moving to a new place, meeting someone old or new, doing something different. Here are some affirmations to help empower you:

I am strong and capable and I have been training for this.

I can overcome any obstacle. There is nothing to fear.

I am ready for real change and I welcome it with open arms.

Affirmations for Dating Confidence

Who doesn't feel worried when going on a date? Even if we are ready to find a new partner, we are often intimidated and limited by our own beliefs and self-esteem. We are worried about what the other person thinks about us. Here are some affirmations that can give you that confidence boost:

I deserve love and I am confident that I will find it

Dating is fun, even if it does not go the way I planned

Every date is an adventure and I will have fun

I will meet the right partner at the right time

Affirmations that build belief in prosperity

Because the world we live in measures success by how much money we make, it is easy for us to think we are unsuccessful or that other people are doing better than us. We think these thoughts no matter how great our life is and the things we actually have. Though that, wanting more money is not wrong. Having more money means having the ability to get a better house, or a better car or better opportunities for education, or simply a better life. If prosperity and abundance are what you need, here are some affirmations to believe in:

I am moving closer to a life that brings in new opportunities for better income

I am excited to be part of this new investment opportunity

I will get what I want because I worked hard for this. This prosperity is mine.

Bottom Line

Apart from practicing these affirmations, you can also support your self-esteem and belief with other techniques such as meditation and yoga to rewire your brain and focus is towards success in any way or form you want. Simple exercises like affirmations can enable you to reconnect with parts of yourself that you know you deserve better.

Chapter 13: Medications And Natural

Remedies

I wished many times there was a magic pill I could take to chase away anxiety and depression forever, never to haunt me. Yes, there are substances that can work instantly to temporarily take my problems away. Medications from the benzodiazepines group could numb my senses in a matter of minutes. A glass of wine can give me an illusion of escape. But what about side effects? These remedies are potentially addictive. I was always acutely aware of anything that may cause addiction and avoided it as much as I could. Even when I was prescribed painkillers after a few surgeries that I had, I used the bare minimum for fear of getting addicted. Tranquilizers may calm acute anxiety, but I did not want to rely on them long-term.

A group of medications called SSRI (Selective Serotonin Reuptake Inhibitors) are often prescribed to patients suffering from anxiety and depression as a long-term solution. It takes time for such medications to accumulate in a patient's body. Correcting the chemical imbalance in the brain takes some time. It took about two weeks for me to feel the full effect of an SSRI medication I was prescribed. It did take the edge off my anxiety, but I felt odd, as if sitting in a jar of cotton balls. My feelings were so cushioned, they were almost non-existent. I welcomed the relief from acute anxiety, but didn't like the lack of other emotions. More than ever, I was committed to finding other solutions and therapies. I was on a path to healing, determined to eventually lead a happy, anxiety-free and, if I could, medication-free life. I didn't want to endure side effects for long but rather, to help my body produce its own serotonin as well as mood-boosting endorphins.

I was positive these natural methods and therapies were out there for me to find. Once I realized I could improve my situation by educating myself, I was filled with hope. Finally, I saw light at the end of the tunnel I was stuck in and was ready to peruse everything available for my healing.

Research

I have to admit I didn't use the Internet much in my research. There are a couple of reasons. First, I have a tendency to "get lost" in virtual reality and barely resurface for air. There were times when I was highly addicted to surfing the net and checking into social media for hours at a time. That had to change, so I limited my time on-line only to necessary e-mail checking a few times a week. With internet research, I often had trouble staying focused on only the question at hand and hours later would find myself reading some totally unrelated article. I also can't trust everything I read on-line and it takes too much extra time to verify information. For me, books and magazines were much easier to manage and trust.

To sum up, I aimed to be a well-educated patient. I became informed on diet and supplements that affect the mind-body connection. I observed my own body's reaction to various stressors and foods.

Dopamine and Serotonin

A chemical imbalance in a person's body can wreak havoc on his emotions. There are various ways to restore this balance. Correctly prescribed medication as well as supplements, herbs, diet and exercise prove to be beneficial. There are also numerous coping mechanisms that can stabilize the release of dopamine, serotonin and endorphins to make us feel significantly better in shorter periods of time. With time, I assembled quite a list of potential stress-reducing remedies. I sought a way to wellness with minimal side effects. I was so weary of pain that I often didn't apply only one method to wait and see if it worked. I used various relaxation techniques and remedies simultaneously. Looking back, I think I should have waited to see what worked best, but I was desperate. Through trial and error, I sifted through various remedies to reduce overall stress and anxiety symptoms and found what works best for me. It took me a long time to pinpoint the best ways to stop anxiety from taking control over my body and mind and become paralyzing. I could choose from deep breathing, laughing or a call to a girlfriend for a fun chat. Then there are stress-reducing techniques such as acupuncture, diet adjustments, and regular workouts, to name a few. The mind-body connection never ceased to fascinate me. We truly are wonderfully made!

Preventative Medicine and Conventional Medicine

These two should work side by side. I was fortunate to have a family practitioner that was knowledgeable not only in conventional therapies but also in preventative and alternative medicine. I saw this doctor on a regular basis for over a year. She was the one who prescribed my SSRI and Benzodiazepine medications and gave me so much good advice. She gave great recommendations, adjusting medication and supplements, and suggested various non-traditional methods of medicine, mainly for relaxation purposes. But she didn't specialize in psychology, naturopathy or acupuncture, so my quest continued. Only later did I discover herbs and supplements that worked even better for me than conventional medication.

Drugs: Pros and Cons

For months I refused to take any SSRI drugs. I refused to accept that my condition was merely a deficiency of Prozac or some other medication. Eventually, I succumbed but it took some convincing from my doctor to try one. I was not aware then of the majority of other therapies. In my case, taking medication worked, and I stayed on it for nine months, being closely monitored by a doctor. It made a big difference in my life. If you know how depression feels, let me tell you, it is as if my world was like the beginning of "The Wizard of Oz" movie, and then, after a couple of weeks of taking ten milligrams of meds a day, it slowly turned into a Technicolor rainbow—colors and feelings I missed for months. I experienced joy again.

The SSRI medication I was prescribed didn't work right away. It had to build up in my system gradually, which took about two weeks. Then the heaviness of anxiety slowly lifted. I experienced a slight mental fog, but still better than a sense of hopelessness and overwhelming fear I experienced for far too long. I thought I could stay on this medication for a while, but only a definite period of time seemed agreeable to me.

Side Effects

There are numerous other possible side effects listed for anti-anxiety medications, including nausea, stomachache, and even suicidal thoughts. Another side effect that is not often talked about is a loss of libido. While singles that practice abstinence may welcome it, for married people it may cause extra discord of relationships already affected by a mood disorder.

Mood-altering medications and supplements made me drowsy. I also experienced extreme vivid dreaming. Not that I had too many nightmares, but in the morning I could recall more dreams than usual and it was hard to get up in the morning. I was tired, did not feel well-rested and energetic and could not wait for the time when I did not need to take anything.

Many people I talked to have been taking mood-altering medications for years. For me, the main side effect, even with a small dose, was losing my senses overall. I felt as if I was slowly moving through a light cloud, which was uncomfortable and I knew I couldn't tolerate that for long.

It was crucial to ask questions about all drugs prescribed and my experiences with them, including contraindications. But taking myself off medication without a doctor's supervision could have made matters much worse. Unlike many other drugs, SSRI accumulate in the body over time, and abruptly quitting them may wreak total havoc on the system, so the patient needs to wean from them slowly. Nowadays there is a wide array of medication available to treat mental conditions, and an experienced doctor will find the correct one and adjust the dosage according to the patient's needs and reaction.

Trial and Error of Medication: Adjustment Doctors run tests, ask questions, observe patient's behavior, then write a prescription. I was curious to know which ones of the most popular I'll get: Zoloft,

Xanax, Lexapro or the grandpa of them all: Prozac. My doctor's choice was Lexapro. As far as I know, there are no definitive tests to pinpoint the exact medication and dose that a patient needs. A doctor will use his expertise and guidelines, prescribe a particular medication, then observe how it works and make adjustments as necessary. Some conditions may require a cocktail of meds, but in my case, I did well with what I tried first, although mild side effects convinced me to get off it as soon as my doctor approved. When my doctor thought I was ready to get off my medication, she gradually decreased my dosage until I was free to live without it. I still had a prescription for Lorazepam, which works very fast, but only to be used on occasion of acute anxiety.

I was eager to emerge from the thin layer of brain fog into a bright light. At first my senses were not as sharp as they used to be before the illness and I still experienced ups and downs, but I was not afraid. I wanted to live to the fullest without being numbed. I was longing to regain my life and to learn to correct occasional chemical imbalances in the most natural way possible. I even sought out controversial treatments.

Medical Marijuana

For centuries opium, marijuana and other plant-based concoctions were used to treat a wide range of maladies. In the past, even opium and cocaine were prescribed as remedies for various diseases. After it was discovered how addictive these substances are and how damaging they can be to one's health, they became outlawed. Nowadays there is a lot of disagreement about the use of medical marijuana and its healing properties. At the risk of controversy, a little explanation may cause opponents to change their minds. Currently, there is more research being conducted by the FDA on the healing properties of cannabis (medical marijuana). This herb is not just being used as a "sinful potion," even though many know it as an illegal drug solely used to get high or feed an addiction. Have you not also heard of people becoming addicted to pharmaceutical painkillers? Addiction can sprout from various sources. Some people get addicted easier than others, for whatever reason, and in such cases psychological help is necessary.

In some states, medical marijuana is legal and has been used successfully to treat patients with cancer, chronic pain, Post Traumatic Stress Disorder and anxiety. Medical marijuana may help patients get rid of pain that otherwise can only be helped by strong medications with damaging side effects.

I thought for a person with anxiety there may be relief from taking certain herbs and this particular one as well. I was willing to give it a try, obtained a prescription and found out that for me it didn't work the way I was hoping. I expected to become pleasantly relaxed, but I experienced brain-fog that I disliked, and my anxiety didn't disappear, though somewhat decreased. With marijuana, it is hard to control the intake of cannabis, whether it is smoked or consumed in treats; it is also hard to predict how it will affect a person. There are a few varieties that supposedly affect patients differently. After a few tries, I gave up on this remedy and moved on to other ones, as it did not help. It is possible that I was so afraid to get addicted that my body did not accept it as a potential remedy. Thus, the search to finding effective natural remedies continued after this detour.